Social Skills and Langauge Development Activities

Magic Circles for Children
Pre-K through Second Grade

Gerry Dunne, Ph.D.

Cover: Dave Cowan

Copyright © 2013 by Innerchoice Publishing • All rights reserved

ISBN - 10: 1-56499-089-3

ISBN - 13: 978-1-56499-089-1

INNERCHOICE Publishing
15079 Oak Chase Court
Wellington, FL 33414

www.InnerchoicePublishing.com

Illustrations may be reproduced in quantities sufficient for distribution to children in programs utilizing *Social Skills and Langauge Development Activities*. All other reproduction, in any manner or for any purpose whatsoever, is explicitly prohibited without written permission. Request for such permission should be directed to INNERCHOICE PUBLISHING.

How the Circle Became Magic

A young child gave the Magic Circle its name. At the close of a circle session, he proclaimed:

This was just like magic! I said something and so did everybody else.
And we all listened! It's a "Magic Circle".

Contents

Early Childhood Development and the Magic Circle 1

   The Social-Emotional Development of Children in Preschool and Kindergarten 1
   Goals, Benefits and Structure of The Magic Circle 12
   The Social-Emotional Themes of the Magic Circle 14
   How to Lead a Magic Circle 16
   The Magic Circle Promises 16
   Steps in Leading the Magic Circle Session: 19
   Questions and Answers about Implementing the Magic Circle Program 22

Unit I – Self Awareness 24

   Finding Out Who We Are and What We Can Do

      "I Can Say My Name" 25
      "I Can Point to the Parts of My Body" 27
      "I Can Draw a Picture of Myself and Tell You About It" 28
      "I Can Show You Something I Can Do with My Body" 29
      "I Can Move My Body to Music" 31
      "I Can Relax My Body" 32

Unit II – Self Management 34

   Expressing and Enjoying Our Talents

      "I Can Act Like a Favorite Animal" 35
      "I Can Paint a Picture and Tell You about It" 36
      "I Can Play a Musical Instrument" 38
      "I Can Sing a Song" 40
      "I Can Make Something Out of Clay" 41

Unit III – Social Development and Responsibility 43

   Relating Responsibly with Others

      "I Can Greet You" 44
      "I Can Thank You for Doing Something I Liked" 45
      "I Can Say Something Nice to You" 47
      "I Can Tell You What I Like about Your Picture" 49
      "I Can Show How I Answer the Door" 50

Unit IV – Self Awareness 52
Using and Enjoying Our Senses

- "Something that Tastes Good".. 53
- "Something that Smells Good" 55
- "Something I Enjoy Hearing" 57
- "Something that Feels Good to My Fingers" 59
- "Something I Enjoy Seeing".. 61

Unit V – Self Management 62
Showing What We're Learning

- "I Can Show You Where Things are Kept" 63
- "I Can Use Things" 64
- "I Know Some Color Names"... 65
- "I Can Sort Things into Groups" 67
- "I Know Some Letters of the Alphabet".. 69
- "I Know Some Numbers" 70

Unit VI – Social Development and Responsibility 72
Cooperating with Others

- "I Can Serve You" 73
- "I Can Share a Treat with You" 74
- "I Can Share a Tricycle with You" 75
- "I Can Pick Up Blocks with You" 76
- "I Can Carry a Table with You"... 77
- "I Can Help You with Your Jacket" 78

Unit VII – Self Awareness 80
Experiencing and Expressing Our Feelings

- "I Can Show You Something in the Room that I Feel Good About".................... 81
- "Something in the Box that Gives Me Good Feelings" 83
- "I Can Show You Something from Home that I Feel Good About" 85
- "Something I Do at School that Makes Me Feel Good"...................................... 86
- "Something I Do at Home that Makes Me Feel Good" 87
- "A Favorite Place Where I Feel Good" 88

Unit VIII – Self Management 90

Taking Pride in Our Accomplishments

- "A Game I Learned to Play" 91
- "A Time I Took Care of Myself" 93
- "I Thought I Could Do It and I Did" 95
- "A Time I Kept Trying and Then I Could Do It" 97
- "A Time I Did It All By Myself" 99
- "A Time My Mistake Helped Me Learn" 101

Unit IX – Social Development and Responsibility 103

Understanding and Caring for Each Other

- "An Animal Liked What I Did" 104
- "A Person Liked What I Did" 107
- "Things People Do that Hurt Others" 110
- "Things People Do to Create Anger in Others" 113
- "How I Stay Safe at Home" 116
- "How I Stay Safe Away from Home" 120

Early Childhood Development and the Magic Circle

Between the ages of two to five life is very exciting! The world continues to be a complex and mysterious set of structures young children are only beginning to comprehend, but that doesn't bother them too much. What matters is their own explosion of power! Their feelings are "raw."

Why Do Small Children Do What They Do?

Most adults have spotty memories of people, places and events that occurred during their early years, but many of these are remembered because of their novelty. For example, we recall the time we fell down the back stairs which resulted in iodine on two skinned elbows or how Mom reacted the time we got caught picking peaches from the neighbor's tree. But the underlying themes of our lives, our deep inner strivings, are usually not recalled for being the serious matters they were. To understand who we were then and how we struggled as only a small child does, we turn to the theories of developmental psychologists. Then many things about ourselves start to become clear, things we had never figured out before.

It's the same with small children we know and love. Their actions often mystify us. What's going on inside them is often unreadable because it's been so long since we grappled with the serious developmental tasks of early childhood ourselves. The key to understanding and working with our young charges comes in the form of developmental theory, a fascinating collection of well-researched ideas.

Basic Needs

Before we discuss psychological development let us take a moment to state the obvious, yet sometimes overlooked point: *psychological development is secondary to biological development.* In other words, human beings can only grow and flourish emotionally, mentally, and socially when their physical development is unfolding properly. Our theories in developmental psychology apply to human beings (young and old) who first and foremost have had their needs adequately met for physical safety, nutrition, warmth, exercise and rest.

Here's another fundamental point: *in order for psychological development to unfold young children must have a psychologically safe and supportive environment.* They must be accepted and cared for by their caretakers. They must be protected, but not overprotected, so they can develop their own powers. Their struggles must be taken seriously and respected. That's why parents and teachers of small children can best love and support them when they know what their inner strivings are and how to create nurturing and stimulating environments for them.

The Social-Emotional Development of Children in Preschool and Kindergarten

Let's briefly summarize the challenges, or "work," all human beings face from birth through five years of age. It's important in this discussion that we get back to birth because a key tenet of human development theory is that *development is cumulative*. This means the issues of infancy, (birth to about two years of age) although they may have been resolved to the appropriate level for the individual before turning three, still matter in a variety of ways throughout the rest of his or her life. This concept also means that the work done in one stage of development prepares the individual for the challenges of the next. Success at one stage sets the tone for future success; difficulties and failures take their toll at future stages.

Besides the developmental challenges of infancy we will also talk about the inner strivings of early childhood (about two to four years of age) and middle childhood (about five to seven years of age) in this section.

Here we will focus on the inner developmental struggles of preschoolers and kindergartners. In his book, *Childhood and Society,* the renowned psychologist, Erik Erikson calls each of these struggles a "psychosocial crisis," and assigned one to each stage in the life cycle. Therefore, we will discuss three psychosocial crises: one for infancy, one for early childhood and one for middle childhood. Additionally, we will examine the four developmental tasks for each of the first three stages of life, twelve tasks in all, with attention to how educators and parents can assist and support the child as he or she faces each one. Finally, we will point out some of the ways in which this guidebook addresses the psychosocial crises and developmental tasks of the first three stages of life by stating some of the pertinent Magic Circle processes, tasks and topics it offers.

The Magic Circle Process Model

A repetitive activity we call "the Magic Circle" can be very meaningful to small children. Magic Circles are carefully structured, safe social environments wherein children can perform tasks, express themselves verbally, and receive positive acknowledgment for these actions and expressions without being put down. With older children we call this process The Sharing Circle.

We will describe the goals, benefits and structure of the Magic Circle in more detail in the next section

Infancy
Birth to about Two Years of Age

During the first two years of life human beings do enormously more learning and growing than in any other two year period! Underlying all this growth is the challenge to develop trust in people, primarily caretakers. This emotional development is relatively easy when the people in the baby's life show him love, talk and sing to him and meet all of his or her physical needs. Mistrust is the tragic result when the baby's caretakers neglect or abuse him. People who have developed more mistrust than trust in infancy are at a great disadvantage throughout later life because effective human relationships are very difficult and sometimes even impossible for them. By contrast, the baby who learns to trust his caretakers is positively set for the challenges of early childhood and beyond.

Because "Trust versus Mistrust" remains a critical issue for preschoolers and kindergartners (as it does for everyone at all stages in the life cycle) this guidebook offers Magic Circles which address the issue of trust.

Four developmental tasks are undertaken by infants.

Object Permanence. According to Jean Piaget at approximately the ninth or tenth month, infants become aware that objects in the environment do not cease to exist when they are out of reach or view. If an object is removed from the infant's view and searching behavior occurs, you can conclude the baby has developed this concept.

Babies cannot become aware of the independence of objects around them, including people, without becoming aware of themselves as separate entities at the same time. Thus, the development of object permanence is also the beginning of self-concept in that babies come to recognize themselves as the origins of their own actions. The attainment of this concept frees them from total reliance on what they can see. Piaget explains that the ability to hold the image of an object or person in one's mind is the first step in complex representational thinking, an essential element in the development of logic and reason.

Caretakers can support the development of object permanence by providing infants with a stimulating sensory environment and by introducing novelty from time to time. Since preschoolers and kindergartners are still actively involved with the task of holding objects in their minds, this guidebook offers Magic Circles with such topics as: *"Something I Enjoy Seeing," "I Can Show You Something in the Room that I Feel Good About,"* and *"I Can Show You Where Things Are Kept."*

Sensorimotor Functioning and Primitive Causality. Once a baby knows that objects and people do not cease to exist when they are not in sight (object permanence), the stage is set for the first level in the development of intelligence. "Sensorimotor functioning" refers to the infant's increasing ability to interact with, and explore, the environment. His or her actions become increasingly differentiated, diversified and coordinated. In this pre-language state, concepts are built through infants' continuous perception and investigation of their surroundings. For example, a baby may retrieve an out-of-reach object by pulling it toward him using the blanket upon which it rests. "Primitive causality" refers to the ability a baby develops to associate specific actions with regularly occurring outcomes, for example crying to elicit needed attention.

Caretakers can support the development of sensorimotor functioning and primitive causality by providing babies with a variety of interesting, but safe, manipulative objects; adding more complex stimuli to the environment; providing more opportunities for autonomy; ensuring success; and encouraging greater tolerance for frustration. Babies also need for their caregivers to initiate interactions with them instead of solely responding to their needs for attention.

Since preschoolers and kindergartners are still actively involved with motor functioning and making an impact on the environment, this guidebook offers Magic Circles with such topics as: *"A Game I Learned to Play," "A Time I Kept Trying and Then I Could Do It,"* and *"I Thought I Could Do It and I Did."*

Maturation of Primary Motor Functions. Infants rapidly develop patterns of muscle coordination from head to foot which are essential to the continuous development of their intelligence. Significant motor achievements during the first two years are coordination of the sucking response, holding up the head, rolling over, reaching and grasping, sitting, crawling, standing, walking, and running, all of which facilitate the infant's exploration of the environment. As infants gain greater mobility and control in their worlds, being free to explore and experience varied stimulation and pursue goals, feelings of competence are developed as well.

Caretakers can support the maturation of primary motor functions by providing a stimulating environment including manipulative objects and by encouraging motor exploration. Babies need to struggle and practice these new activities without being pushed or held back.

Since preschoolers and kindergartners are still actively involved with the development of motor functions and learning about their bodies, this guidebook offers Magic Circles with such topics as *"I Can Point to the Parts of My Body." Motor tasks such as those entitled "I Can Show You Something I Can Do With My Body,"* and *"I Can Relax My Body"* are also offered.

Social Attachment. The process by which babies develop positive emotional relationships with the significant people in their environments is known as "social attachment" or "bonding."

Babies demonstrate the formation of social attachment by being able to differentiate between significant people and others by acting more relaxed and comfortable when "attached" people are present and more fretful in the presence of non-attached persons; trying to maintain contact with significant individuals; and becoming distressed when these people leave. To attain and preserve closeness with a significant person, infants at first suck, grasp, smile, cuddle and follow the person with their eyes. Later they purposefully seek attention and physical closeness.

Caretakers can support the development of the critically important task of social attachment with infants by consistently meeting their basic needs for physical care, security and emotional closeness. Babies need to be held, cuddled, rocked in the arms, talked and sung to daily. *It is on the basis of this social learning that all later relationships with people are formed!*

Preschoolers and kindergartners are still very much involved in forming social attachments with others (caretakers and peers). For this reason Magic Circles are offered in this guidebook as the primary process model because they offer an affirming social environment in which healthy attachments can be readily formed when conducted on a regular basis. Magic Circles offered which relate to the task of social attachment are: *"I Can Greet You"* and *"I Can Say Something Nice to You."*

Early Childhood
About Two to Four Years of Age

For those children who have successfully met the developmental tasks of infancy, every day is full of discovery and exciting possibilities during early childhood. They are resilient and learn fast. The name of their game is control; they want to do everything they can "all by themselves."

Erikson states that this need to develop independence and competence is of critical importance to human beings in the early years with severe consequences if it is thwarted. Young children create positive images of themselves as separate and effective persons if they are consistently given affection and allowed to experience success in new endeavors. Their self-esteem is established and they will confidently interact with others, tackle new challenges and develop new skills in the years ahead.

If, however, small children are neglected or emotionally abandoned they will develop feelings of shame in themselves. If they are constantly discouraged, criticized, and/or experience repeated failure at tasks attempted, it is likely they will develop doubt about their abilities.

The Magic Circle process which is offered consistently throughout this guidebook addresses the needs of small children to develop autonomy by giving them the opportunity to express themselves verbally in any manner of their choosing (as long as they do not say anything hurtful to anyone). Most of the Magic Circle tasks and topics in the curriculum offered herein begin with the words, *"I can..."* which address the child's growing needs for competence and independence. Additionally, some topics directly address autonomy, for example: *"A Time I Took Care of Myself,"* and *"A Time I Did it All By Myself."*

Four developmental tasks are undertaken during Early Childhood.

Use of Language. Perhaps no other developmental task of the early years is as impressive as the innate human ability to learn to speak. This achievement generally occurs between the ages of sixteen months and age three and progresses by age four to a vocabulary of about one thousand words and the correct use of basic grammatical sentence structure. It is made possible not only through imitation, but also through the use of originality and problem-solving skills.

Piaget and Inhelder refer to the development of articulate language as one aspect of the pre-operational thought stage, involving the child's ability to symbolically represent something such as an object or concept in his or her mind. *In other words, the development of intelligence and language go hand-in-hand!*

As small children begin to organize their worlds and translate thoughts into meaningful sentences understood by others, a sense of accomplishment develops. They realize that through language, much information can be gained about the world, and others can be influenced to respond to their needs. They also learn that language is a key to friendship.

The development of language in small children can be supported most effectively by educators and parents when they frequently converse with the children and encourage them to hold conversations with each other. These verbal experiences strengthen not only the development of language, but also thought, which contributes to the child's ability to be more self-controlling. It is important to use concrete terms and normal inflection and pronunciation as in adult-to-adult conversation when talking to small children. They should never be "talked down" to.

Oral language is the principle mode of expression of Magic Circles. By speaking to their fellow circle members (peers and leader) and by listening to what others have to say, children's growing abilities to verbally communicate are utilized and strengthened. Verbal expression is then built upon to inspire other forms of expression including art, reading, singing and drama. Additionally, a specific Magic Circle topic in this guidebook which focuses directly on the value of speech is: *"I Can Say Something Nice to You."*

Initial Development of Self Control. Young children begin to learn self-control along two dimensions; the first being the management of their emotional impulses and the behavior spurred by those impulses. The initial emotional responses of very young children are uncontrollable; immediate gratification of needs is the primary goal. If demands are not met, then intense frustration and anger are aroused. Gradually, however, if their needs are usually met in a timely fashion small children learn to delay gratification and the intensity of their emotional reactions are usually reduced.

Educators and parents can support the development of self control in small children by modeling appropriate and rational handling of their own emotions. They accept the feelings of young children, but redirect children's angry outbursts into constructive outlets. When adults request young children to delay gratification they should also be sure to supply the gratification later as promised.

The process of the Magic Circle helps children delay gratification for immediate attention. They must wait for their one turn to speak to the topic during the session (if they wish to take it) by raising their hands and being called on by the leader. Additionally, the *Magic Circle Promises* stipulate that no one will interrupt anyone else. Although these procedures and rules are very prone to be disregarded by small children when Magic Circles begin, the children are gradually and consistently trained to honor them through positive reinforcement for desired behavior.

Additionally, children need to develop an awareness and respect for their own feelings in order to begin the lifelong challenges of emotional self-understanding and self-control. Magic Circle topics which directly address the children's feelings are: *"A Favorite Place Where I Feel Good"* and *"Something I Do at School that Makes Me Feel Good."*

The second aspect of self-control in small children emerges as they discover their growing abilities to affect and control objects and events around them. They strive to do what they see others doing and may be given a chance to make their own decisions about such matters as what to draw, play, wear, eat and verbally share in the Magic Circle. When their imitative actions are appreciated and their decisions respected, young children develop confidence in themselves as their abilities and skills become more complex.

Educators and parents can support young children to develop this aspect of self control by allowing them to make constructive choices within carefully structured limits and then to honor the children's choices. Adults should also notice and appreciate children's efforts and accomplishments, continuing to offer more complex tasks that they can handle. It is important to display a respectful recognition of the attempt to succeed whenever children try something, but fail. It is particularly helpful for adults to convey the attitude that mistakes are a natural part of the learning process.

The Magic Circle process allows children to imitate the leader and other children in their adherence of the promises to respect each other. As noted, they may decide for themselves what to say when it is their turn to speak or even if they wish to take their turn. Specific topics which relate to their abilities to affect and control objects and events around them are: *"I Can Use Things"* and *"A Time I Kept Trying and Then I Could Do It."*

Use of Fantasy and Play. At about the age of two, small children develop the mental capacity to recall events and imitate people and things not immediately present. At first such imaginative repetition is a mere replay of what has been observed or that with which the child is familiar, such as pretending to drive a car.

Later the play theme becomes more imaginative and symbolic. The childhood game of playing "house" is a familiar example in which children use their own experience as a base, creating unique situations which express their view of themselves within the family setting. This kind of imaginative play serves as an outlet for the expression of inner feelings and wishes.

During this symbolic play stage, children may also create "imaginary friends" who serve the purpose of keeping them company when alone, and being confidantes for their private expressions. Imaginary friends may also become convenient scapegoats on which children can project responsibility for their own misdeeds.

Educators and parents of small children can support the development of the use of fantasy and play by first being aware of the importance of this developmental task in children's lives. Fantasy and play permit small children to feel more masterful over the limitations their developing speech imposes on them. It not only frees them from total dependence on verbal communication, but also from the frustration of trying to fit the expression of their feelings into existing words and phrases. Adults should not seek to limit or meddle with the imaginative expression of small children unless their behavior is in some way destructive. Rather, children should be given opportunities and encouragement to exercise their budding creative, imaginative powers.

As an accepting social environment, the Magic Circle is a setting for creative verbal expression. Both the realistic and imaginative verbal offerings of children are respected. A Magic Circle task in this guidebook which elicits an imaginative response is *"I Can Act Like a Favorite Animal."* A topic which spurs children to create an object in their imaginations is *"Something in the Box that Gives Me Good Feelings."*

Self-Locomotion Skills. The term "toddler" indicates the importance of locomotion skills at the earliest stage of this development series. By the age of three, however, the young child no longer toddles, but walks more gracefully and effectively. In general, the child's personal sense of mastery is heightened by the development and use of a number of more agile locomotive skills which bring her into closer contact with the environment. As walking is mastered, other locomotor skills are added; running and jumping emerge first, followed at age four by leaping. Running ability continues to improve with repeated practice and is valued for its own sake as well as for its usefulness in games.

Children of this age are eager to use their bodies in various ways and will easily learn skills requiring large muscle coordination such as swimming, skiing, dancing and sledding. Riding a tricycle which provides movement, speed, thrill, independence and social ties for the child, has an important psychological significance. It is one of the future objects which will symbolize increased independence from the family and a source of identification with peers.

Educators and parents of small children can support their development of self-locomotion skills by providing a safe, spacious environment with equipment for the practice of running, climbing, sliding, pedaling, dancing and swimming. It is particularly important that adults not push young children to perform actions they are not ready for, nor hold them back. Adults can also perform a vital function by noting the development of these skills and making positive comments to the children.

Magic Circle tasks which encourage small children to use and enjoy their developing self-locomotion skills are: *"I Can Share a Tricycle with You," "I Can Carry a Table with You,"* and *"I Can Move My Body to Music."*

Middle Childhood
About Five to Seven Years of Age

Exuberance for life begins to be more refined when youngsters reach the middle childhood stage of development. They continue to discover and delight in their new abilities, but now they want to know more about the world. They are eager to learn as much as they can about all facets of their existence. Concurrent with their eagerness to learn, children who have not attended preschool now find themselves in a new environment created for that very purpose—kindergarten. Here, other people besides parents become key figures. As they interact with their teachers and peers, children find out how much and in what ways they are valued. These learnings, in turn, strongly influence their estimations of themselves.

Five to seven year olds who developed high degrees of trust in infancy, and autonomy during early childhood, are bound to become curious investigators during middle childhood. Strong initiative can be seen in children with high self-confidence. Initiative in children fosters a shifting of their attention from complete focus on self-discovery to active cognitive inquiry and investigation of the external world. When this curiosity and investigation are respected and reinforced by adults, children's intelligence and self-regard are strengthened. When adults brush off children's questions and repudiate their investigative activities the usual result is guilt. Thus, significant adults are in a position to mold a creatively open child or one with an anxious dread of novelty.

Educators and parents who wish to support the development of initiative within five to seven year olds need to be patient, understanding and appreciative, often very difficult challenges. Children need attention, acceptance, appreciation and affection; they also need socialization and discipline.

Magic Circles are an approach to meeting these needs simultaneously. The structure of the circle consistently provides each child a turn to perform or speak, to observe and listen to others, to respond to those others and to discuss what he or she learned. Everyone abides by the Magic Circle Promises to observe and listen respectfully. No one is allowed to interrupt, probe or put anyone else down. Specific Magic Circle topics offered in this guidebook which allow children to tell about learnings they have achieved are: *"I Can Use Things," "I know Some Letters of the Alphabet," "I know Some Numbers,"* and *"I Know Some Color Names."*

Four developmental tasks are undertaken during Middle Childhood.

Sex-Related Identification. The name of this task does not adequately reveal its complexities. If children are to positively form their identities as males and females during middle childhood, they must do much more than learn to apply the appropriate gender label to themselves. They must also identify with the same sex parent, learn to prefer being the sex they were born, and acquire an understanding of appropriate behaviors for their gender. There is little controversy about the first three of these challenges, but the last one has become a much-discussed issue in recent years.

By the time children are two and one half years old they have correctly learned to identify themselves as boys and girls. This ability is the result of listening to what their parents have told them: *"What a good boy!" "That's my girl!"* Later children develop an identification, primarily through imitation, with their same sex parent and internalize this parent's values and attitudes.

Whether a child's parents value strict adherence to traditional sex role standards, or not, the child will be exposed to such standards at school, from the media and through other channels of the culture. Although such traditional standards have been generally relaxed in many families, by the middle childhood stage most children have acquired a great deal of information about these sex-linked expectations.

Where traditional sex-role standards are rigidly imposed the themes of dependence and aggression play influential roles. Typically, boys are permitted and in some cases encouraged, to be aggressive and discouraged from being dependent, while girls are often reinforced for dependent behavior and not often reinforced for aggressiveness.

Educators and parents can support the development of sex-related identification in children by making positive references to children's genders in conversations with them. It can be explained matter-of-factly to boys that they are becoming men like their fathers and uncles, and to girls that they are becoming women like their mothers and aunts. Adults should do their best to model their finest qualities and characteristics to children of the same sex in order to enhance their appreciation of their gender. Whenever possible children who are missing a parent of their own gender should be exposed to appropriate models of that gender.

Only those sex-role standards should be imposed on children that will help them be accepted by others but not preclude their growth and development. It is unhealthy to rigidly expect aggressive behavior in boys while disapproving of their dependent behaviors and to expect dependent behavior in girls while disapproving of their shows of aggression. All children naturally have both dependent needs and the desire to take bold steps at times. To deny them these modes of expression (as long as no one is getting hurt) may preclude their full development.

It is important that children not only prefer being the sex they were born, but to learn to respect and not fear or dislike, persons of the other sex. This lesson is probably best learned by children when they observe adults of both sexes relating to each other in friendly, respectful ways.

The Magic Circle is helpful in promoting children's identity because it operates in such a way that each child's individuality, which includes gender expression, is honored and respected. At the same time the Magic Circle promotes equality. No one is permitted hostile or overly aggressive behavior, nor denigrated for dependent behavior. As a result of regular participation in Magic Circles assertive behavior, a healthy alternative to aggressiveness and submissiveness, tends to be developed in circle participants.

Concrete Mental Operations. Beginning with middle childhood and continuing into the late childhood stage, children develop a qualitatively new form of thinking. At this stage children begin to recognize the logic and order of the physical world and realize they can predict physical events. Three of the most important conceptual skills achieved are referred to by Piaget as (a) classification, (b) conservation, and (c) combinatorial skills.

Classification may be thought of as "the backbone of intellectual functioning." It involves the child's ability to classify objects and events according to a common category or class. Children who have developed this skill are able to clearly differentiate between parts and wholes, or groups and subgroups. For example, they can demonstrate the knowledge that elemental subclasses, such as chihuahuas and great danes, can be included within a broader category: dogs. This ability to classify and differentiate demonstrates the mental capacity to hold a concept in mind and make a series of decisions based on that concept, an ability that assists in problem solving.

Conservation involves the child's new ability to comprehend the idea that quality and quantity remain constant with respect to volume, weight, area or number, despite perceptual changes. For example if a liquid from a medium-width jar is poured into a narrow jar, the child at the former pre-operational level of thinking will only be able to predict correctly that the liquid will be higher in the narrow container than in the medium one. But the same pre-operational child is also likely to think that the narrow container contains *more* liquid because it is higher. It is only when children reach the concrete operational level of thinking that they understand the *amount* of liquid *stays the same* when poured from jar to jar. Children who do not yet "conserve" depend on their perceptions to make judgments and are not yet able to resist perceptual cues that suggest physical changes when no such change has actually taken place.

Combinatorial skills embody the child's ability to manipulate numbers. During this stage the mathematical skills of addition, subtraction, multiplication and division are learned. The child possesses the ability to arrange objects in quantitative terms, a conceptual skill Piaget called "seriation" and identified as critical in understanding the relationship one number has to another. The concrete-operational child has the capacity to solve problems by considering the relative relationships between them, such as: *"If A is smaller than B, and B is smaller than C, is A smaller than C?"* Once the concepts governing these operations are understood, they can be repeatedly applied regardless of what specific objects or quantities are involved.

Thinking at this stage begins to acquire many of the characteristics of adult thought, but the reasoning processes of five to seven year olds are still limited to dealing with *concrete* objects and events. They are as yet unable to coordinate thought processes in terms of abstractions, a skill which develops in Piaget's next and final stage of intellectual development, the formal operational period.

Educators and parents need to be aware that the development of concrete operational skills is a child's bridge to understanding the world more fully and to answering his or her pressing questions. It is, therefore, crucial to his or her lifelong mental functioning. For this reason children should be afforded numerous and varied educational experiences of a concrete and tangible nature in keeping with their ability to understand.

It is also extremely important to allow children to develop concrete operational thinking skills according to their own individual learning timetables. For this reason, educators and parents need to be particularly careful not to push children beyond their ability to perform or hold them back by withholding new challenges.

Children should be frequently reinforced in the form of positive comments as they master new concrete operational tasks, verbally noting their specific accomplishments *regardless of how they compare with other children in their age range.* (The most beautiful flower in the garden is not necessarily the first to bloom.) Such comments promote their self-esteem and encourage them to develop further.

With it's emphasis on reinforcing children for their growing skills and abilities the Magic Circle highlights for them the value and importance of their own physical, emotional, social and intellectual development. The Magic Circle task, *"I Can Sort Things into Groups"* directly addresses the concrete mental operation, classification. Additionally, responding to topics which address specific aspects of their own experience calls forth similar abilities within children to classify. Examples of such topics are: *"Something that Tastes Good," "Something that Smells Good,"* and *"Something I Enjoy Hearing."*

Early Moral Development. There are several schools of thought regarding the manner in which moral development takes place in human beings. The Cognitive Developmental Approach places the emphasis for moral development on the child's thinking processes. It assumes that as children grow older, they are increasingly able to make moral judgments on the basis of the more abstract and logical dimensions of a situation. This approach to moral development, elaborated by Lawrence Kohlberg, and based on the general cognitive development theory formulated by Piaget, hypothesizes that children progress through three increasingly complex, sequential, developmental, and qualitatively distinct levels of moral reasoning, each level having two substages. No stage can be skipped, but individuals may stop or regress at any point.

According to Kohlberg's theory and research, the child before the age of ten uses moral reasoning at the preconventional level which includes two sub-stages. At the first sub-stage (punishment/obedience) children perceive morality in terms of actions and their external consequences. They explain the reasons for their behaviors in terms of rewards or punishments. At the second sub-stage (instrumental relativism) children are more concerned with satisfying their own needs and desires. They may cooperate with others, but generally do so to get what they want.

Kohlberg theorizes that individuals do most of their moral reasoning at one stage while reasoning to a lesser degree at the stages they are leaving or advancing toward. Thus, some children during middle childhood are beginning to comprehend the second level of moral reasoning (the conventional level) and its two sub-stages. At the first sub-stage of the conventional level, children's moral decisions are greatly influenced by the evaluations and opinions of those who they view as important people, primarily parents, teachers, and peers. At the second sub-stage they explain their behavior in terms of rules or prescriptions for actions set by society and/or the peer group.

It is interesting to note that, according to Kohlberg's theory and research the post-conventional level of moral reasoning does not develop until late adolescence (about eighteen to twenty-two years of age). At this level individuals develop an awareness of the relative nature of values and commit to a more universal or global set of moral principles.

Educators and parents can conclude that the most obvious implication of the three foregoing stages of moral development is the importance of modeling moral behavior and giving careful moral guidance to children. Adults should refrain from doing anything in front of children they would not like to see them repeat. It is important to talk with children frequently about why certain actions are right and others are wrong but it should be done in reasonable and concrete ways.

The manner in which adults discipline children also has an impact on their developing moral codes. The most effective discipline techniques in teaching morality are those which help children: (a) control their own behaviors, (b) understand the effects of their behaviors on others, (c) determine more acceptable behaviors for future instances, and (d) enlarge feelings of empathy for the victims of their misdeeds.

Magic Circles operate as settings for character development because the rights of every circle member are actively and consistently respected. Children are directed to employ self-control and considerate behavior (to wait their turn to speak, to listen to others, to keep from bumping others, etc.). Specific tasks for Magic Circles in this guidebook allow children to "try on" certain pro-social behaviors, such as: *"I Can Say Something Nice About Your Picture," "I Can Serve You,"* and *"I Can Share a Treat with You."* (An important point about these tasks is that each child not only offers the action to another child, but receives the action from the other child as well allowing the natural outcome of reciprocity in human interactions to be directly experienced.) Additionally, a variety of Magic Circle topics herein address themselves to the ways in which people affect each other with an emphasis on kind behavior and empathy for others' feelings. Such topics include: *"A Person Liked What I Did,"* and *"Things People Do that Hurt Others."*

Group Play. During middle childhood, children still engage in individualistic free play and fantasy play, but they also begin to show an interest in a new form of play. They want to participate in more structured group games, ranging from such simple activities as "Duck Duck Goose" to more complex and competitive sports like kickball and soccer.

Group play involves the more complex cognitive and physical skills evident at this stage. It provides peer cooperation and interaction, and furnishes children with opportunities to develop increasing awareness of the many different perspectives of other participating children.

Educators and parents need to be aware that children at this stage engage in play primarily for the enjoyment it provides. Winning is not the major goal. Children's developing muscle coordination and mental development can be facilitated by introducing them to new games that gradually involve increasing cognitive complexity and physical skills. Their natural growth in understanding teamwork can also be facilitated by positively reinforcing their cooperative behaviors and de-emphasizing the competitive aspects of each game.

It is important for adults to encourage and reinforce children to involve themselves in body movement and play solely for the pleasure they provide. Adults should provide, or frequently transport children to, an enriching physical environment including obstacle courses, ropes, rings, hoops, balls and ample space. It particularly delights children when adults join them in play.

Although the Magic Circle is primarily a setting for serious, but enjoyable, verbal interaction where everyone is seated most of the time, certain aspects of the developmental task, group play, are addressed anyway. Because cooperation and fairness are emphasized in the circle, educators have noted how often children carry these standards into games on the playground. In fact, the consideration and empathy children gradually learn in the Magic Circle after experiencing regular sessions over an extended period of time seems to set the tone for the ways they interact with each other in general. Specific topics in this guidebook which relate to group play and the value of cooperation are: *"A Game I Learned to Play,"* and *"I Can Pick Up Blocks with You."*

How Educators Foster Social-Emotional Development in Young Children

We have discussed the first three developmental stages in the human life cycle; Infancy, Early Childhood and Middle Childhood, and the developmental "work" done during each stage. What does this information tell us as educators? Let's take a moment and talk about our influence in the overall development of the children in our counseling settings and classrooms.

Numerous professionals have pointed out that children are primarily affected by their parents and families outside the school causing them to wonder how much impact they can make. It was in response to this concern that the Magic Circle Program was first developed and has grown to become a vital part of thousands of school counseling and classroom programs all over the world.

The Magic Circle creators and consistent users of the program believe that children's mental, emotional, physical and social development is highly dependent on the treatment they receive from *both* educators and parents. We believe that both are enormously influential in structuring the children's world which reflects to them who they are and how they function. We believe this because we have personally seen and experienced the positive lifelong effects of the efforts of skilled and caring counselors, teachers and others in the lives of students. In many cases those students came to school from dysfunctional homes.

Educators are in a position to consistently guide children into novel experiences as the children demonstrate readiness and then provide attention and positive feedback to them in order to help them recognize their own capabilities. Teachers and counselors have the capacity to perform in this manner because they are with the children three to six hours a day, one hundred and eighty plus days a year. In order to provide these attitudes and concepts to children educators are most effective when they utilize a carefully structured, systematically organized curriculum.

In the next section we will explore in more detail how the Magic Circle Program assists educators in their efforts to foster child development.

Goals, Benefits and Structure of The Magic Circle

In order to help educators make as much positive impact on children's overall development as possible the Magic Circle curriculum has been designed to combine a number of concepts from developmental psychology along with sound educational principles and practices. Concepts from the psychoanalytic and behavioral schools of psychology have also been included. This curriculum features, but is not limited to, the Magic Circle, a structured, yet not overly complex process model. Through its process and content the Magic Circle addresses a number of human needs and growth issues simultaneously in an economy of time. Let us now go into more detail and discuss how these ends are accomplished by the program.

First, the Magic Circle is a small-group, structured social environment wherein all participants share equal status. Even the leader is a participant. Emotional safety, security and comfort are assured as life issues are discussed, social skills are practiced, and self awareness is developed. This occurs because no one is pressured to do anything in the circle except listen respectfully to others. In addition to listening, participants are invited to respond to the specific task, or topic, for the session on a voluntary basis. Each individual has the free choice to decide what to do, or say, for him- or herself. The Magic Circle Promises (ground rules) stipulate that there will be no interrupting, dominating, probing, criticizing, or gossiping.

Although a different task is undertaken or topic discussed in each session, the Magic Circle process remains the same. After a few sessions, children learn what to expect and what is expected of them. This provides a sense of security and control which allows them to think and interact with one another regarding the task or topic without wondering what's going to happen next. In such a setting attitudes and concepts are best internalized while effective oral communication and listening skills are practiced.

The Magic Circle process promotes self-understanding and self-respect as well as understanding and respect for others. As the children express themselves and observe and listen to the leader and the other children and teacher in the circle, they gradually realize all human beings are alike, in that everyone senses, feels, thinks, and behaves. At the same time it becomes obvious that people are different from one another because each individual senses, feels, thinks, and behaves in his or her own unique fashion. This understanding, referred to as the Principle of Unity and Diversity, is central to mental health. Children who develop this awareness know and like themselves as themselves. Beyond that they can know and like others for themselves.

Oral Language: Key Mode of Expression

As we noted in our discussion regarding oral language development in Early Childhood in the former section, the small child's rapid acquisition of vocabulary and use of correct grammar in speech is impressive. Indeed, oral expression is the first language form human beings use, laying the foundation for such later forms as reading and writing. Throughout most people's lives, oral language is used far in excess of any other form of communication. Because of these factors, and because the development of oral language and intelligence go hand-in-hand, carefully guided activities utilizing oral language are of great value to small children.

As the key mode of expression in the Magic Circle, oral language is engaged in with enthusiasm because children are enabled to talk about their own experiences, as opposed to making forced or "canned" responses or repeating phrases generated by someone else. Thus the development of oral language is strengthened and refined through its utilization.

An Integrated Language Approach

Educators regularly capitalize on the connections and integrations between different subject areas and functions. In doing so, the curriculum is enriched and children realize how learning and experiencing in one realm can help them gain competence in other realms. An Integrated, or Balanced Language Approach to learning is one of the most vivid examples of integrating learning experiences as opposed to separating (fragmenting) them.

We believe oral language is a key which unlocks the door to Literacy. As many educators have discovered, one of the most exciting aspects of oral language is its power to stimulate other forms of expression. Children readily engage in reading, drawing, acting, playing games and singing songs when they can read, draw, dramatize, play, and sing about things they chose to talk about first and vice versa. The Magic Circle may be used as a catalyst to an Integrated Language Approach to learning.

At the end of each Magic Circle in this guidebook related activities are suggested including reading, drama, art, games, and songs. Each activity offered has a theme which is closely related to the Magic Circle it follows. For example, after the task, *"I Can Move My Body to Music,"* the "Hokey Pokey," a song and dance which also allows the children to identify the parts of their bodies is suggested.

Many of these related activities involve reading (in unison or being read-to by an adult). This is the most natural way for children to learn to read. The process builds on itself as the leader invites children to comment (verbalize further) on what they have read, and others have said, drawn, acted, or sung. Thus, an integrated approach to language literacy is fostered using the Magic Circle as the central, unifying activity.

Effective Communication Skills

Many individuals have mastered oral language, but are actually poor communicators. They may be able to speak well, perhaps even eloquently, but the fact is: effective communication is not assured by effective oral language. In its most basic form we define effective communication as having two aspects. These are: the ability to speak in such a manner that all of one's thoughts are accurately and concisely conveyed verbally and non-verbally to others; and the ability to listen to the content of another's verbal statements and observe his or her non-verbal messages without becoming confused by interferences from within.

By participating in the Magic Circle, children are not only encouraged to use and strengthen their oral language abilities, but to become effective communicators as well. Children who have had the opportunity to participate in regularly conducted Magic Circles over the course of several months have often demonstrated outstanding communication skills because they have practiced these skills over and over again in the circle.

When speaking in the Magic Circle, children are enabled to verbally respond to the topic in a manner of their own choosing without distractions. At times they are assisted to clarify points and/or elaborate by the leader's use of open-ended questions. Additionally, they are frequently enabled to receive feedback giving them an idea of how well they conveyed their message verbally. This occurs when a review, an optional feature of the Magic Circle, is conducted by the leader. The review is never a judgment on the quality of the child's statements. Rather, it is simply a neutral repetition, or summary, of each speaker's remarks. To be reviewed-to in this manner is very reinforcing to the child who spoke. It says to her, *"You were worth listening to and I understood what you had to say."*

When listening, children are directed to give attention to the speaker and accept his or her verbal contributions without interruption or comment. If the leader conducts the optional review, each child has at least one opportunity to repeat to another what he or she heard the other say. Thus, listening skills are sharpened, practiced and reinforced.

The Social-Emotional Themes of the Magic Circle

Let's return to our focus on early childhood developmental theory and research discussed in the prior section. In doing so we find many important developmental areas and many of these are addressed through the Magic Circle. The first of these themes conveys how fundamentally important it is for children to know who they are as unique and special individuals. This theme can be identified as self awareness. Another theme relates to the vital need for children to see themselves as becoming increasingly competent and able to manage impulses, demonstrate self-discipline and self-motivation. Yet another area is a recognition of their social nature as human beings and calls for the development of effective social skills and empathy for others. In order to address these key concerns of Early Childhood Development the Magic Circle curriculum has been organized around these basic themes of self awareness, self management, and social development and responsibility.

Self Awareness

As the label suggests this area refers to what individuals know and understand about themselves. It is a natural outgrowth of how well they have succeeded in past developmental stages of their lives and how well they are succeeding in their current stage. People with a healthy and accurate self awareness know themselves well as they really are.

Small children start out not knowing very much about themselves. They learn who they are and what they can do by constantly trying new experiences and satisfying their curiosity. From this ongoing process children form their self-concepts based on the information they obtain by themselves and from others. When children are generally appreciated they learn more about, and appreciate, themselves. When they are generally criticized and interpret that criticism to mean they are not acceptable they are prone to distort reality about themselves. The Magic Circle is a time and place where children get to explore their inner thoughts and outward actions in a safe, supportive, and affirming environment which promotes their growing self awareness in a positive way.

Children who have developed a realistic level of self-awareness are at a distinct advantage because they know and accept themselves. From the understanding, patience and feedback they have received primarily from adults they learn easily what's going on in the exterior world and they know what's going on within themselves. They realize that they, as human beings, feel, think, and behave. As they grow and develop they become increasingly aware of how these separate functions within themselves influence each other. The more self-aware and positive about oneself children are, the more they are likely to have the ability to control their impulses. In other words this lifelong challenge can begin in early childhood when children are developing self awareness.

Instructional units, tasks and topics in this guidebook are presented in order to develop self awareness and foster a realistic, yet positive, self-concept in small children. These focus the children's attention on their *self-image, senses and feelings* — three cornerstones of human experience.

Self Management

Managing one's feelings and behaviors, and liking oneself and having confidence in one's abilities are key elements in development. Children with high self-management skills enjoy using and taking pride, but not inflated pride, in their developing skills. They also have a growing ability to identify feelings and regulate accompanying behaviors in a pro-social manner.

The Self-Management units in this guidebook have been designed to help young children develop these skills by offering Magic Circles with "success tasks" and topics which focus on effective functioning. The tasks are structured so as to assure each child a successful experience with a chance to talk about the good feelings that success brings. The tasks also serve as a vehicle to give each child deserved positive feedback immediately after his or her successful performance. The Magic Circle process also provides a continual practice in impulse control as the children have to wait for their one turn. They also must listen and not interrupt the speaker or disrupt the circle process. As they adhere to these rules, they receive positive feedback for their behavior and over time this self-management and impulse control is likely to become internalized.

Social Development and Responsibility

Learning to communicate and cooperate effectively with others and to empathize with their feelings are the themes of the Social Development and Responsibility units in this guidebook. By participating in these activities children are given the opportunity to discover for themselves the personal rewards that frequently result from kind and responsible behavior.

In addition to practicing effective and considerate forms of social interaction while participating in the circle, children are also given a chance to talk about social dynamics at a level relevant to them. This dual focus is particularly powerful in allowing children to develop effective social skills such as listening, cooperating and caring. They are also likely to understand the benefits for behaving in these ways.

A key aspect of the Social Development and Responsibility units is to provide an initial understanding to children that they are personally influential in the lives of others. They can affect others positively or negatively depending on their actions. This seemingly obvious fact is frequently missed by many people of all ages, especially young children who are usually caught up in reacting to the behavior of others while rarely considering how their own actions have affected someone else.

How to Lead a Magic Circle

More than anything else, the Magic Circle is a structured, organized event that allows for spontaneity in the moment. This event is somewhat formal, yet enjoyable, and follows the same set of rules and guidelines each time it occurs. No two Magic Circles are the same, however, because each one has a different topic, or task. Additionally, you and the children are different, due to influences affecting you between sessions.

Sometimes referred to as a "listening laboratory," the Magic Circle combines several educational approaches to simultaneously achieve the overall objectives of increasing children's self awareness, self management, social awareness, and relationship skills. Included in the process are the circular small group seating format; ground rules (the Magic Circle Promises) setting the tone for positive interaction and emotional safety; a procedural structure inviting each child to show a skill or verbally share, give and receive reflective feedback, and to cognitively summarize learnings gained.

The purpose of the Magic Circle is to allow participants the opportunity to verbally explore aspects of human life with each other; appreciate themselves and each other as developing persons; practice effective communication skills; and develop empathy for others.

Does this mean that leading a Magic Circle is difficult? No. Counselors and teachers already have all the skills needed for this role.

These skills include: following curriculum guidelines; stating and enforcing simple rules of considerate conduct; modeling one's own respect for these rules; leading a discussion; verbally communicating with children in clear, non-patronizing language; and listening carefully to what children say while responding appropriately. When you lead a Magic Circle you are a leader, model, coach and co-participant all at the same time.

First, let's cover the Magic Circle Promises. Otherwise known as "The Ground Rules," the Magic Circle Promises are an extremely important part of the Magic Circle because they clarify appropriate and inappropriate behavior. Because of the universal nature of each promise, learning the promises not only equips a child for effective participation in a Magic Circle, but in most life situations involving people as well.

The Magic Circle Promises

- *We will just bring ourselves to the circle and nothing else.*
- *Everyone gets one turn.*
- *We don't have to take a turn if we don't want to.*
- *We will listen to the person who is speaking.*
- *We will stay in our own spaces and not bother others with our hands or feet.*
- *We won't interrupt, or put anyone down.*

Let's consider each Magic Circle Promise from two vantage points: why it has been included and how to enforce it.

- ***We will just bring ourselves to the circle and nothing else.***

This promise allows the children to tell themselves and each other that they, as themselves, are sufficient offerings to the group. Their presence, thoughts, feelings and experiences are important. Therefore, just bringing themselves to the circle is all that's necessary.

This promise also let's the children know that material objects should be left behind and not brought to the circle. By honoring this promise, distractions are minimized because the children will be prone to focus their attention on you, and each other, instead of the objects in their hands. Whenever children do bring objects to the circle, gently ask them to place the objects under their chairs, or behind them if they are seated on the carpet. (Occasionally, the circle task itself, does involve objects. When this occurs, ask the children to remove the items from their hands in a similar manner until it is time for them to hold and discuss the items.)

- ***Everyone gets one turn.***

Whether a topic, or task, is featured in the Magic Circle, this promise lets the children state their knowledge that they will be included. Everyone will be given a turn, an equal opportunity to participate (speak and/or perform) because each individual is just as important as everyone else.

The word, "one," is very important here. When children are allowed more than one turn in the Magic Circle, the session becomes difficult to manage. The tone of equality is also sacrificed. This comes about when children who enjoy talking and performing vie with each other to gain your permission for additional turns. As this occurs, these children take up the allotted time with as many turns as they can obtain causing reviews and summaries at the end of sessions to receive less time and attention.

Sometimes, the more outspoken children attempt to influence the more reserved and reticent children to give them their turns with the result that some children have no turn while others have several. With the allotment of one turn to share, the more outspoken children gradually realize that they need to mentally organize what they have to say before speaking because they will only have one chance. At the same time, the less outspoken children gradually realize that they are just as important as their more gregarious peers and their contributions are just as valuable.

Do not allow the children to take more than one turn during a Magic Circle, even if a child contributes very minimally when having his or her turn and seems more prepared for a second opportunity. If children beg to take a second turn, or ask their peers for their turns, explain to them that they may not have another turn, even if some children take no turn. It's like dividing a pie into as many pieces as there are circle members. Everyone gets a piece whether he or she chooses to eat it or not. When Magic Circles are conducted on a regular basis, the children will come to realize that they will get another turn in each upcoming circle.

- ***We don't have to take a turn if we don't want to.***

This promise assures the children that no one will be pressured to speak, or perform, in the Magic Circle if she prefers not to. Because each circle member is valued for simply being present, and because each individual's privacy is honored, the children may individually choose to contribute by observing and listening anytime they wish. They are free to volunteer to speak to a topic, or perform a task, or not.

The most effective way to enforce this promise is to model it. Allow the children to volunteer to take turns during the Magic Circle by suggesting they raise their hands when they are ready to contribute and then calling on them. If some children have not raised their hands after all of the others have had their turns, yet they look eager to participate, gently invite them to take a turn: *"Sally, do you have something you'd like to say?"* If the child demurs, accept the response with the same acceptance you would show a child who shares.

If one child demands that another speak, or perform, remind her that the child will let us know if he wants to take a turn.

- **We will listen to the person who is speaking.**

By stating this promise the children are reminding themselves that they will receive everyone's attention when they are taking their turn. This includes giving you attention when you are clarifying the topic, or task; leading the review; or asking summary questions.

The most effective way to teach children to give others attention and to listen carefully to what they are saying is to model doing it yourself. When some children are not listening to the one who is speaking, encourage them to do so by acknowledging those children who are giving the speaker their attention: *"Good for you Carlos. I noticed how you looked right at Judy and listened to her as she spoke."* As soon as a child who has difficulty listening does so, be sure to reinforce him or her.

- **We will stay in our own spaces and not bother others with our hands or feet.**

As the children state this promise, they recognize the importance of respecting each individual's physical space and physical being. This is a very important ground rule because it prevents the major distractions that result from annoying body contact, a violation that makes the Magic Circle less enjoyable for everyone. Most importantly, when young children are taught this self-management behavior, they are practicing and learning very important aspects of self control and management of impulses.

The best way to deal with this violation is to prevent it. By making this promise the children are taking a first step toward managing impulses. Additionally, your praising commentary to the group about how well they are doing to keep this promise curtails many distractions that unwelcome physical contact brings. For example: *"I'm very impressed with how you are all staying in your own spaces today. This way we can have a fine Magic Circle."* You can also separate troublesome pairs when the group sits down or place yourself between them.

At times a child will blatantly poke or kick another. When this occurs remind him of the promise. If the child persists remind him again. Only as a last resort ask him to leave the circle and to sit down in a specific spot such as a "thinking chair." If you can, continue the session with him present, perhaps having him change places with another child. Then speak to him privately afterward: *"Hank, I need your help. I want to have good Magic Circles, but it's hard when you keep poking the person next to you. Everyone looks at him and at you and forgets what we're doing. I want you to stay in the Magic Circle because we get to know you better when you are with us. But we can't have you there if you keep poking other children. Will you help?"* If the child still persists, give him something to do that is less desirable to him during the next Magic Circle and explain why he is being excluded. Later approach the child and tell him you missed him and ask him if he would like to come to another session. If the he says yes, make sure he knows that he must not bother other children with his hands or feet as a provision of participation.

- **We won't interrupt, or put anyone down.**

This is another very important promise that also teaches self control and self management. Like annoying physical contact, interruptions and put downs are very distracting and disruptive to the Magic Circle. They are capable of entirely changing the tone from a supportive, enjoyable atmosphere to one of confusion and disharmony.

By making this promise, the children are taking the first step to prevent the damage that these violations can cause. Your careful modeling also has a powerful influence on the children. By demonstrating attention, acceptance and appreciation to every child, your behavior sets the tone and is imitated more and more by the children as your Magic Circles occur.

Frequently make general statements of acknowledgment to the group when they honor this ground rule: *"I've noticed something. No one has interrupted anyone else during this Magic Circle. Isn't that great?"* or *"You know, I want to tell you how good I feel about our Magic Circle today. Everyone is treating everyone else well today. Doesn't that make you feel proud?"*

If a child does interrupt, or put another down, determine her conscious or unconscious motive before you decide what to do. If the action was designed to gain attention reward it with as little attention as possible. Tell the child: *"Johnny is speaking, Susan. Remember the promise not to interrupt?"* or *"Please don't say things like that, Wally. That's a put down and it can make another person feel bad about you."* Deliver these words with a cool tone, low energy and minimal eye contact. When you do look into the child's eyes do so flatly.

If attention for herself is not the motive a child has for interrupting or putting another down, deliver the words above in a more energetic (perhaps even warm) manner. Perhaps the child simply wants to make contact with the individual she has interrupted, or put down, and has seen other people become involved with another person using these means.

Now, let's cover the specifics of effective Magic Circle leadership at each point during the session.

Steps in Leading the Magic Circle Session:

First, let's list the steps. Then we will discuss each one.

> 1. *Gather the children into the Magic Circle and set a positive tone.*
> 2. *Review the Magic Circle Promises.*
> 3. *State the Magic Circle topic, or task.*
> 4. *Give each child who volunteers a turn.*
> 5. *Conduct a review (optional).*
> 6. *Ask some summary questions.*
> 7. *Close the circle.*

1. Gather the children into the Magic Circle and set a positive tone. Begin with very cooperative, yet expressive children. As you draw the children into the circle and encourage them to make it circular so that everyone will be able to see everyone else, communicate a welcome to them non-verbally. Through your eye contact, smile, gestures, etc., let each individual child know he or she belongs to the group and you are looking forward to hearing what each one may have to say. Your enthusiastic, yet serious, attitude at this point says to the children: *"This is an important time. We are going to learn about ourselves and each other. It's going to be interesting and fun."*

2. Review the Magic Circle Promises. In your first few Magic Circles tell the children the promises and discuss them briefly. In subsequent sessions, ask them to see how many of the promises they can remember. Or ask the children to individually tell the group which promise they particularly like. In this manner, you are not "laying down the law," but allowing the children to state their own promises to each other. From time to time as the promises are reviewed, concentrate on one promise and then another, creating a more in-depth understanding of the reason for each promise. As the children gradually demonstrate behavior consistently respecting the promises, dispense with these discussions except for occasional reviews on an as-needed basis.

In addition to discussing the promises at the beginning of a Magic Circle session, it is equally important, as leader, to enforce them just as you enforce other rules during classroom activities.

3. State the Magic Circle topic, or task. About half of the Magic Circles in this guidebook feature topics and the other half feature tasks. Topics are responded to by the children with verbal sharing; tasks call forth "performances" and involve verbal commentary. Whether you are stating one or the other, generally think of this as having four parts, as follows:

A. *State it (topic or task).*

B. *Elaborate / demonstrate.*

C. *Restate it.*

D. *Provide silent time for thinking and preparation.*

In each lesson we suggest ways to introduce the Magic Circle throughout this guidebook, but you know best how to communicate to your particular group of children, so please don't simply read what we've written verbatim. State the topic, or task, and elaborate on it in *your own words.*

The goal in stating the topic, or task, is to clarify to the children what the Magic Circle session is about and what is expected of them if they wish to participate. It is important, therefore, when you elaborate to "speak children's own language" to them but not in a simplistic, patronizing manner. The intention is to eliminate confusion and assure the children they can succeed if they volunteer to take a turn. The better teachers do in stating topics and clarifying/demonstrating tasks, the more likely the children will understand and respond effectively during the Magic Circle.

Providing silence for thinking and preparing is a "mental time out" for everyone. It has the effect of adding a note of relaxation to the session. At the end of the silent thinking time, most children are centered and ready to share and listen.

No matter how tempted you might be to change to another topic, or task, if the one you have offered doesn't seem to be going over well, *don't do it*. The reason for this recommendation is that every topic and task can be responded to and found to be worthwhile. Some are more challenging than others and some are more fun than others, but each one relates to some aspect of life and is worthy of attention. If you generally expect the children to respond they will. But if you keep changing the topic, or task, it's a way of saying, "I'm going to keep on trying to please you until I get you to say something." This, of course, is an unwise manipulation. It contradicts the promise that assures the children the right to participate simply by observing and listening if they so choose.

4. Give each child who volunteers a turn. Generally known as the "participation phase" of the Magic Circle, this period of time is devoted to allowing each child, and you, to take one turn to respond to the topic, or task. This is the "feelings aspect" of the Magic Circle when circle members perform the task, or tell each other about their experiences, thoughts and feelings in response to a topic. All this is to be conducted in an atmosphere of acceptance and support. It is most important that this aspect of the circle be completely free of judgment, advice, or any other sort of distracting or negating commentary even when the children copy each others' responses or state fabrications of reality.

During this time give each child who wishes to respond the chance to do so. When necessary you may assist individual children to make successful verbal contributions by asking open-ended questions, but do so sparingly. During this phase of the session you are also modeling how to keep the *Magic Circle Promises* and enforcing the promises as necessary. Thank the children individually after they have taken their turns.

5. Conduct a review (optional). This is the only optional aspect of the Magic Circle and, as such, is offered at your discretion. Sometimes you have time for it and the group's attention is optimum. Other times you may deem it undesirable. Before we talk about how to lead a review let's clarify what it is and why we do it. We will also discuss how it can go awry.

The review is a Magic Circle phase occurring right after the participation phase. Every circle member who wished to contribute has had a turn and the review simply offers each individual who contributed a chance to hear another circle member tell her what he heard and/or saw her contribute. *It is a simple reflection and that is all.*

The purpose of the review is threefold: (1) to sharpen listening and observation skills, (2) to give each circle member another chance to participate verbally, and (3) to assure the speaker that she was listened to and observed. When we are listened to and observed carefully, we feel valued and when we find out what we heard and saw was accurate, we feel confirmed. Thus, the review helps develop effective communication skills as well as self-esteem.

The review is not an interpretation, an evaluation, or a chance for the reviewer to tell his own related story. None of these approaches enhance the self-esteem of the individual who is being reviewed to. In fact, they are often deflating. They are also time consuming.

Initiate a review by saying: *"Let's review to each other what we heard each other say. I'm going to pick Susan and review to her. Susan, you told us about...(brief summary of Susan's remarks). Did I hear you right?" Now who would like to pick someone and tell him, or her, what he or she, said? Don't worry if you don't remember it all. We don't want to take too much time for this. Besides, we will all help each other remember. Okay?"* Proceed in this manner until every circle member who took a turn during the participation phase is reviewed to, including yourself.

There are a variety of ways to conduct the review. You can name a child and ask, *"Who remembers what Janet told us about and can tell her?"* Then name another, until every child who took a turn has been reviewed to. Or you could conduct the review as a chain wherein the child reviewed to turns to another and reviews to him. He then picks another, etc., until everyone who took a turn has been reviewed to.

6. Ask some summary questions. The summary is the cognitive portion of the Magic Circle. During this phase, the leader offers thought-provoking questions for free-flowing discussion. We have offered two or more summary questions to spark discussion for each Magic Circle in this guidebook, but at times you will probably generate questions more appropriate for the level of understanding for your group of children.

It is important you not confuse the summary with the review. The review is optional; the summary is not. This is because the summary meets the need people of all ages have in varying degrees to find meaning in what they do. Thus, the summary serves as a necessary culmination to each Magic Circle by allowing the children to clarify the key concepts they gained from the session.

At first young children are unprepared to respond to the summary questions. (For this reason, the question we usually offer first in this guidebook—*"What did we do today in our Magic Circle?"*— is easy to answer and invites responses to the next, more challenging questions.) We suggest you assist the children as much as you can to understand the questions and respond to them successfully, but not to tell them what they think or what they learned. Rather, tell them what *you* think and what *you* learned. For example, if you ask: *"Is it okay for you to be different from other people?"* and they do not respond, or say no, tell them: *"I think it's okay for me to be different from other people and if you are different from me that's okay."*

As the children experience more and more Magic Circles and are presented with the summary questions over a period of time, they gradually learn to understand and respond to them. After awhile their summary discussions will be impressive.

7. Close the Magic Circle. Due to the formal nature of the Magic Circle, it should never be left without official closure. This is best done by thanking the children for their cooperation and announcing that the circle is closed. You might also wish to tell them the topic, or task, for the next session and when it will be held.

Questions and Answers about Implementing the Magic Circle Program

We have discussed your role as leader, model, coach and co-participant when you lead the Magic Circle. Let us now turn our attention to your roles as decision maker and coordinator. To this end, this section addresses frequently asked questions about how preschool and kindergarten teachers and counselors have successfully integrated Magic Circles into their overall programs.

1. Why do Magic Circles? We do similar things all day long.

We certainly agree that effective educators consistently use the same skills and focus on similar tasks and topics as those offered for the Magic Circles in this guidebook. We believe that Magic Circles are still very valuable, however, because they combine so many valuable process and content features in an economy of time. Primarily, the small group in a circle with its formal, yet accepting and safe atmosphere is exceptionally supportive of each child and yields critically important benefits and understandings large group "lessons" do not afford.

Additionally, the Magic Circle operates as a focal, or reference, point in the minds of children when related activities, such as those suggested in this guidebook for each Magic Circle, are offered. The children mentally and emotionally integrate the pictures they draw, songs they sing, dramas they enact, etc. with their personal "real life" experiences in the Magic Circle.

2. How often should I hold Magic Circles with my children?

Ideally, each child will experience a Magic Circle each school day. If this is not feasible, arrange your schedule so that each child will participate in a Magic Circle on a regular, if not daily, basis. Perhaps you can arrange for each child to participate once a week. The key is consistency over a long term as opposed to daily circles lasting a week or two and then stopping. It is also valuable when the children know what days they will have the opportunity to be in the Magic Circle and be able to depend on it. If they know the upcoming topic, or task, it is valuable as well.

3. How many children should be in each group?

Depending on the maturity level of your children and other factors, such as how often you can hold a Magic Circle, the answer to this question varies. The rule of thumb is: include the number you can comfortably handle without losing the attention of the children or the small group feeling. With preschoolers just beginning school you may wish to start with no more than two or three children for your first few sessions gradually increasing the number in each group from four to six. (It's okay not to include everyone at first; you are working up to that point.) Kindergartners who attended preschool may be ready to participate in a Magic Circle with as many as four or five other children at first and by the time a few weeks have gone by the number in each group could be as high as seven or eight children. Generally a very comfortable number of children of any age in the Magic Circle is four to six.

4. What do I do with the children who are not participating in the Magic Circle?

We recommend teachers rotate small groups of children during a regular working period from station to station each day. While one group is participating in the Magic Circle the others are with other adults painting at easels, listening at a listening post, modeling clay, reading picture books alone or in pairs, listening to a story, drawing pictures, and other similar activities.

5. Who supervises each group of children at each station?

When teachers lead the Magic Circle, it's impossible to attend to the needs of the children at the easels, the book corner, and the clay table at the same time. Obviously, having aides helps a great deal, but parent volunteers are also especially useful to assist during this time of the day, as well as children from the fifth grade and beyond who delight in taking on responsibilities of this nature.

6. Is there any special time of year that's best for starting Magic Circles?

The best time to start Magic Circles is the first day of school, but they can be effectively begun at any point.

7. Is there a best time of day to carry out a Magic Circle?

Most teachers and counselors prefer the first part of the morning when the children are most alert, able to think introspectively and share verbally in a straightforward manner. However, others prefer midday and still others successfully hold Magic Circles at the end of the school day as a positive closure.

8. Should I offer Magic Circles in the order they are presented in this guidebook?

We recommend you begin with Unit One because it is introductory in nature. We believe your judgment regarding which unit to offer after that is best because you know your children and their needs and interests. However, if you have no reason to alter the order in which we have presented the units, conduct the activities in the order in which they are presented.

Unit I

Self Awareness

Finding Out Who We Are and What We Can Do

As your children experience this initial unit, they will be given the opportunity to develop a closer and more appreciative view of themselves. This will occur through Magic Circle tasks related to their names, the parts of their bodies and what they can do with their bodies. Other activities, including art, reading, drama, games and music, will also be experienced allowing the children to increase their awareness of the vital areas of identity, physical being and physical functioning. This focus will be personal and reinforcing of the children's developing sense of themselves as individuals. It will also be outer-directed, as each child perceives peers and significant adults explore their own self-images.

Magic Circle Tasks in Unit One

"I Can Say My Name"

"I Can Point To The Parts Of My Body"

"I Can Draw A Picture Of Myself and Tell You about It"

"I Can Show You Something I Can Do With My Body"

"I Can Move My Body To Music"

"I Can Relax My Body"

Magic Circle Task:

"I Can Say My Name"

Note:

This first activity is written with extensive detail and description to provide a full example of the Magic Circle. We invite you to bring your own skills and style to each of these activities and to make them your own.

Purpose:

The children will learn how to conduct themselves in the Magic Circle and experience success while performing a simple task. This initial task is presented in order that the children may respond on a very simple, positive level, while they begin the more complex task of learning the format and expectancies of the Magic Circle. Asking the children to say their names in this first circle and the tasks of the next few sessions may seem overly simple, possibly even mundane. They are, however, important because they allow the children to experience success as well as setting the stage for more challenging circle tasks and topics as well as summary questions to be offered later.

Introduce the Magic Circle Promises:

Before starting this first session, you will need to briefly tell the children how we put magic into our circle by following the Magic Circle Promises. Begin by saying something like the following in your own words: *"Today, and on other days, we will meet in this circle to have fun and learn about ourselves and each other. We will talk and listen. This will be our own Magic Circle. Would anyone like to guess why we will call it a Magic Circle? "*

Allow the children to respond and give positive reinforcement to all of their ideas. Then tell them: *"You have all made good guesses. We will call our circle group the 'Magic Circle' because it will seem like magic how good things happen as we talk and share together. There is another reason that it will be like magic. It's because each time we meet in the Magic Circle we will be following the Magic Circle Promises. Let me tell you what they are."*

State and explain the seven Magic Circle Promises, as follows:

1. We will just bring ourselves to the circle and nothing else.
2. Everyone gets one turn.
3. We don't have to take a turn if we don't want to.
4. We will listen to the one who is speaking.
5. We will stay in our own spaces and not bother others with our hands or feet.
6. We won't interrupt, or put anyone down.

Take a few minutes to discuss these promises, but don't overemphasize them at this point. Better to praise the children during, and at the end of the first few circles and every so often afterward for the good job they are doing in keeping these promises.

Introduce the Task:

Next, introduce today's Magic Circle task by saying:

"Each time we meet we will follow our Magic Circle Promises and we will do something. We will also talk and listen. What we do is called our Magic Circle Task. Our task today will be: 'I Can Say My Name.' Let me show you how we will do it." Start by saying your name: *"My name is _____ ."*

Involve the children:

After you have said your own name, explain to the children that when they are ready they may raise their hand and you will give each of them a turn to tell the group their name. As the children participate give your full attention and then state your appreciation to each one: *"Thanks, (Gary) for telling us your name."*

Conduct a review (optional):

Select a child and say, *"I know your name. It is (Gary). Am I right?"* Then ask: *"Now, who would like to choose a boy, or girl, here in our circle and say, 'I know your name.' Then tell him or her what it is?"* Continue in this fashion until everyone has been reviewed to.

Periodically, conduct a review of this nature so that the children will know others are listening and paying attention to what they say, and do, in the circle. The review also gives children who chose not to speak in the former part of the session a way to participate.

Lead a summary by asking:

1. *"What was everyone who took a turn able to do?"*
2. *"How did you feel when you took your turn and did such a good job of telling us your name?"*

As much as possible, allow the children to supply answers to the questions themselves. Help them focus on their positive feelings about participating and being known by their names. Point out that our names are very special and wonderful. It is good to be proud of our names, to learn the names of others, and to use their names when we talk to them.

Conclude the Magic Circle:

Close this, and every, Magic Circle by thanking the children for sharing and listening and for making the circle a success.

Related Activities:

Obtain a photo of each child in the group. Immediately after this Magic Circle display the photos and label each one with the child's name. With a very respectful tone, view the photos and read the names. As you lead this activity say something positive about a physical characteristic and a personality trait of each child as he or she is focused on by the group.

Gather some of the children (about three or four) together and play the game, "I am _____ and I like _____." Begin by saying your own name and what you like. For example: "I am Mrs. Brown and I like kittens." Then direct the child on your right to repeat to you what you said and then to add his or her own statement. For example: "You are Mrs. Brown and you like kittens. I am David and I like to run races." Continue around the circle with each child repeating what has been said by those who have already spoken. Be sure to assist children, as needed, to guarantee their success and to praise each one for having such a good memory. From time to time play this game, increasing the challenge by increasing the number of participants.

Magic Circle Task:

"I Can Point to the Parts of My Body"

Purpose:

The children will review how to conduct themselves in the Magic Circle and experience success while performing a simple task. Additionally, this circle enables children to develop positive feelings about their bodies.

Review the Magic Circle Promises:

Welcome the children to their second Magic Circle and praise them for the good job they did in the first circle. You will want to continue reviewing the Magic Circle Promises (page 16) for this and the next few circles and periodically thereafter. You may ask who can remember one of the Magic Circle Promises and continue until all six have been reviewed. If you have them listed on a chart, review them from the chart, thus reinforcing the words as well as the ideas.

Introduce the Task:

After praising the children for their attention to the review of the Magic Circle Promises, tell them in your own words: *"Our circle task today will be: 'I Can Point To The Parts Of My Body.' Let me show you how we will do it."*

Involve the children:

Continue by saying: *"First, I will ask you to point to your head. Will everyone in the group do that now? Good, you all did that very well. Now point to your ears; point to your nose, etc."*

Continue until all of the children have successfully pointed to most of the various parts of the body you have named. Praise them as a group for doing so well and then ask who would like to try it on his or her own. Then name five or six different body parts for each child who volunteers. Adjust the task so each child will be successful and praise each one each time he or she makes a correct response. If a child is slow to respond or is incorrect, help him get it right. Remember that all experiences in the Magic Circle should be positive so that the children will feel secure and want to participate.

Lead a summary by asking:

1. *"What was everyone able to do?"*
2. *"How did you feel when I asked you to point to a part of your body and you got it right?"*

Help the children to focus on good feeling words like *"nice," "great," "wonderful," "warm inside,"* and others. Point out how wonderful our bodies are and how lucky we are that each part of our bodies do such a good job for us.

Conclude the Magic Circle:

Thank the children for sharing and listening and for helping make the circle a success.

Related Activity:

Play the game, *"Simon Says"* with the children focusing on the parts of the body. However, instead of playing it in the traditional way which involves a variety of movements, simply say: *"Simon says,'Point to your head.'... 'Simon says, 'Point to your abdomen.'... etc.*

Magic Circle Task:

"I Can Draw a Picture of Myself and Tell You About It"

Purpose:

After drawing a picture of themselves, the children will be given the opportunity to tell about their portrait, (what they are doing, how they are feeling, etc.). These activities enable the children to consider themselves as individual physical persons who do things and feel emotions. They are also enabled to realize that each person behaves and experiences emotions in his or her own individual way which sets the stage for appreciation of diversity and respect for others..

Preliminary Preparations:

Prior to conducting this Magic Circle, have the children draw a picture of themselves. In your own words, say: *"We have all seen pictures of ourselves and we have all seen ourselves in the mirror. I would like you to draw a picture of yourself. Draw a picture of all of you. Include all of the parts of your body. Draw the very best picture of yourself you can. Let me know if you'd like some help"* Collect these, then distribute them one at a time to each child artist as they volunteer to share their pictures in the Magic Circle.

Introduce the Task:

After reviewing the Magic Circle Promises, tell the children: *"Remember the drawings you made of yourselves? Sometimes we call pictures we draw, or paint, of ourselves 'self-portraits.' Today, in our circle we will have a chance to show the group our self-portraits and tell about them. I will go first and show you how we will do it."*

Hold up the picture you have drawn of yourself and say something like this: *"Here is a picture of me. It is my self-portrait. I am happy in the picture. You can tell because I have drawn a smile on my face. I am happy because I have on a new hat, a new dress and new shoes. I am also happy because in my picture I am getting ready to go to a party. Some parts of my body I have drawn are: my head, my arms, my hands and fingers and my legs."*

Involve the children:

Ask: *"Who would like to show us his or her, self-portrait and tell us about it?"* As the children volunteer, hand them their self portraits to show and talk about. If they are having difficulty telling about their picture help them by asking questions such as: *"Can you tell us what you are doing?' "How are you feeling?" "Show and tell us about the parts of your body you drew in your self-portrait?"*

As the children finish, thank them for the good job they did. Then collect their pictures to avoid distractions.

Lead a summary by asking:

1. *"What was everyone who shared today able to do?"*

2. *"How did you feel when you were telling us about your self-portrait?"*

3. *"What feelings did we have that were the same? What feelings did we have that were different?"*

Point out that sometimes we feel the same way other people feel and sometimes our feelings are different. It is okay to feel the same and it is okay to feel different.

Conclude the Magic Circle:

Thank the children for sharing and listening and for helping to make the circle a success.

Related Activity:

Following the circle, make a display of the portraits. Include short quotations from statements the children made during the session. Make a classroom activity out of looking at the display and reading the quotations aloud as a group.

Magic Circle Task:

"I Can Show You Something I Can Do with My Body"

Purpose:
The children will be able to show what they can do with their bodies using a board (or line on the floor). Through this process, the children are enabled to deepen their appreciations for the many ways their bodies can function.

Materials Needed:
Four to six foot 2" x 10" board or masking tape.

Preliminary Preparations:
During this Magic Circle, the children will have a chance to do various activities using a balance board. (If a board is not available you can substitute a strip of masking tape.) Place the board, or strip of masking tape, in the center of the circle. Make sure there is plenty of room for the children to jump over, or fall off, the board without landing on other children.

Introduce the Task:
After reviewing the Magic Circle Promises, tell the children in your own words: *"Today, in our Magic Circle we will be showing each other something we can do with our bodies. We will be doing this using this board (or line). There are many things we can do with our bodies using it."*

Involve the children:
Ask: *"Do you have any ideas about what you could do on the board (or line)?"* As the children suggest ways they can use their bodies on the board, have them individually show the group what they have suggested. Praise each child for whatever degree of success he or she has with the task and ask: *"How do you feel after doing so well on the board (or line)?"* Then ask each one to choose another child to try the same task (by pointing).

Make sure each child experiences success by adjusting the task or helping the child as necessary.

If the children have trouble thinking of a variety of ways to use their bodies with the board (or line), suggest ways yourself and ask for volunteers to try each task. Possible tasks include: running around the board, walking down the board with a partner walking beside them holding their hand, walking the board one foot in front of the other, walking sideways down the board, jumping off the board onto the floor, jumping over the board, sitting on the board with their arms held out and their feet off the floor, etc.

Conduct a review (optional) by saying:
"Let's see how well we can remember what each of us did with our bodies on the board (or line). Who can remember what (John) did? How did he use his body on the board? Let's have someone show us what he did."

Allow the children to systematically select each other and to repeat their actions. Urge them to talk about what they are doing as they do it. Additionally, praise them and ask them to tell how the individual they are imitating said he felt as he performed his task: *"How well you remembered what (John) did. You remembered that he walked the board sideways and only stepped off once. You also remembered how good he said he felt when he was able to do it."*

Make sure each child who performed is reviewed to.

Lead a summary by asking:

1. *"What were we able to do today?"*
2. *"How did people say they felt when they were able to do something with their bodies so well on the board (or line)?"*
3. *"How do you feel inside when someone else does a good job?"*

Point out that our bodies are like wonderful machines; we can make them do so many different things for us. Additionally, guide the children to recognize that not only does it make us feel good to do well ourselves but we can also feel good when we see others doing something well too.

Conclude the Magic Circle:

Thank the children for sharing and listening and for making the circle such a success.

Related Activity:

Take an individual photo of the children as they perform their movements during this Magic Circle. Later, gather them together and show them each photo one at a time. As each child is focused on, ask the group, *"What was (Susan) doing? Yes, she skipped around the line. Here she is skipping in this photo."* Then address the child: *"What was it like for you, (Susan)? How did you feel?"*

Make a display of these photos. Add short captions. For example, under Susan's photo, place the sentence: Susan is skipping around the line. She feels free. Look at the display and read the caption out loud to the group. Then read it aloud together.

Magic Circle Task:

"I Can Move My Body to Music"

Purpose:

The children will be able to show how they can move their bodies to music. This experience enhances the children's growing appreciation of their bodies and what their bodies can do for them. It also allows them to appreciate the physical performances of others.

Materials Needed:

CD or MP3 player, and three to four varying musical selections.

Introduce the Task:

After reviewing the Magic Circle Promises, tell the children in your own words: *"Today, in our Magic Circle we'll be showing each other something we can do with our bodies to music. Let me play a some music so you can feel it."*

Involve the children:

Play a little of the first selection, then stop it and say: *"Does this music make you feel like doing something with your body? Who can show us what you would do? What kinds of movements might you make to this music?"* If the children are reluctant to volunteer, take your own turn and then talk about how you felt about moving to the music.

When you and all (or most) of the children have had a chance to move to the first selection, say: *"Let me play another piece of music while you listen and feel it. Then we'll take turns showing each other how we could move to it."* As the children individually volunteer, have them show the group one way they might move to the music. Praise each child for doing such a fine job of moving to the music and after each performance ask: *"How did you like moving to the music? What kind of feelings did you feel inside as you were moving?"*

Then ask: *"Who else would like to show us a way to move to the music?"*

Follow this same procedure for each of the musical selections. Be sure to praise each child for the creative way he uses his body. Also, give each one a chance to express how he felt during and after the experience.

Conduct a review (optional):

Intersperse the review with the performances by allowing everyone who wants to, to get up at your signal and imitate the child who is performing. Later, ask the children to tell each other what they saw each other do and heard each other say about how they felt as they moved to the music.

Lead a summary by asking:

1. *"What were we able to do today?"*

2. *"How did people say they felt when they were able to do something with their bodies to the music?"*

3. *"How do you feel inside when someone else is doing a good job of moving to the music?"*

As much as possible, let the children supply responses to these questions themselves. Guide them to recognize that not only does it make us feel good to do well ourselves but we also feel good when we see others doing something well.

Conclude the Magic Circle:

Thank the children for sharing and listening and for helping make the circle a success.

Related Activity:

Reinforce the children's developing knowledge of body parts as well as their enjoyment of movement to music by dancing the Hokey Pokey with them. Afterward, hold a free-flowing discussion about how much our bodies can do for us and how enjoyable it is to use them to move, dance and play.

Magic Circle Task:

"I Can Relax My Body"

Purpose:

The children will be able to relax their bodies through deep breathing, tension release and visualization. All of us live in a world of stress and it is important we learn ways to relieve the stress that builds up in our bodies. In today's Magic Circle the children will have a chance to learn ways to relax so they can call upon this skill whenever they choose.

Introduce the Task:

After reviewing the Magic Circle Promises, begin the circle by saying in your own words: *"Today, our Magic Circle task is, 'I Can Relax My Body.' Relaxing our bodies means breathing very slowly and deeply and letting our bodies go very limp. We will begin learning how to relax our bodies by starting with some slow breathing exercises."*

Involve the children:

Begin with the children seated in chairs. Suggest: *"Let's sit back and close our eyes. Breathe in very slowly and hold it, one, two; breathe out slowly and hold it, one, two; breathe in slowly and hold it, one, two; breathe out slowly and hold it, one, two."*

Repeat this breathing exercise several more times and then praise the children for how well they were able to breathe slowly and deeply.

It should be noted that some children have problems attending to quiet times so you may have some who will want to laugh or act silly during these exercises. When this happens, stop the exercise and gently remind the children of the Magic Circle Promises. Then continue with the task. Be sure to pause after each instruction in order to assist the children as needed.

Say: *"You have all done such a fine job of learning how to breathe slowly and deeply. Now we are going to learn how to relax our bodies even more. We'll do this by doing one part of our bodies at a time. First we will make the part tense. Let's begin by closing our fingers and making our hands into really tight fists. Make the tightest fists you can. Now open your fingers slowly and make your hands as loose and relaxed as you can. Make them like the hands of a rag doll. Good! Now tighten your arms as tight as you can. Good! Slowly loosen your arms until they are really relaxed and limp. Let them hang down as loose as you can like the arms of a rag doll. Good!"*

Continue with the legs, feet, neck and face. Then say: *"Now let your whole body be relaxed and breathe slowly and deeply. Imagine yourself as a soft towel or sponge. You are becoming softer and limper and softer and limper until you almost melt. Stay very relaxed and quiet."*

Pause for a few seconds then say: *"Now it is time to wake up all the parts of your body. Tell your feet and legs to wake up as you tighten your legs and feet a little. Tell your arms and hands to wake up as you tighten them a little. Tell your face and neck to wake up as you tighten your head and neck a little. Now that you are all awake open your eyes and sit up straight. You have done very well at learning how to relax. From time to time we will start our Magic Circle by first relaxing our bodies."* (You may want to repeat the exercise with the children lying on the floor. Also you may choose to use this relaxation exercise frequently after the children have returned from energetic outdoor activities and need to calm down.)

Conduct a review (optional) by saying:

"Let's see if we can remember how we relaxed our bodies. Can anyone remember what we did first?" Continue with your questioning, helping the children to be successful in their responses. Then say: *"You did such a fine job of remembering how we relaxed our bodies. Now whenever you feel like relaxing, you know how to do it."*

Lead a summary by asking:

1. *"How did you feel when we were breathing slowly and deeply?"*
2. *"How did you feel when we relaxed each part of our bodies?"*
3. *"Is it good to know how to relax? Why?"*

As much as possible, allow the children to supply answers to these questions themselves. Help them focus on their positive feelings about being able to breathe in general and to slow down their breathing when they choose to relax. Additionally, discuss the value of learning how to relax each part of their bodies in order to calm themselves whenever they choose to do so.

Conclude the Magic Circle:

Close the circle by thanking the children for cooperating with you as you showed them some of the "secrets of relaxation."

Related Activities:

Conduct a guided imagery exercise with the children. First, direct them to lie down on the carpet and close their eyes. Next, guide them through the same relaxation process they experienced in this Magic Circle (slow and deep breathing followed by deliberate and systematic tensing and releasing of the tension in each body part). When they are completely relaxed, slowly and soothingly suggest they imagine they are in a wonderful place like a beautiful park. Suggest they visualize a variety of stimuli such as birds flying, rain softly falling, the sun bursting through the clouds, a rainbow, etc. End the exercise gently and then talk about it as a group.

Provide art materials and suggest the children draw some of the things they imagined in the guided imagery exercise, such as the birds they heard singing, or the rainbow they saw. Some children may just want to draw lines and colors to represent the experience they had. As the children create their pictures, comment to them about how good they are at imagining and drawing the pictures they created in their minds.

Later, when the group reconvenes, ask the children to take turns telling about their pictures as products of their imaginations. Make a display adding captions that are direct quotations from the children. Then view the display and read the captions together.

Unit II

Self Management

Expressing and Enjoying Our Talents

According to Webster's Scholastic Dictionary, a talent is "a special faculty." In this unit the children will be invited to demonstrate the special faculties they are developing in the enjoyable realm of the arts. A major purpose of this unit is to give each child the opportunity to celebrate his or her own growing abilities, and those of his or her peers, to paint, sing, play an instrument, draw, sculpt and act. To be succinct, the primary purpose is to enhance each child's self-esteem and self-efficacy. The Magic Circles in this unit are, therefore, structured toward the end of giving each child a success experience. We call these Magic Circles "success tasks."

Your personal directions and commentary while presenting these activities are of great importance. Begin by giving very clear directions. Always demonstrate the task through to completion before the children take their turns, explaining how it should be done. By knowing what is expected the children are more likely to volunteer to take turns.

Another vital key to making this unit work is to gear each activity to the performance level of every child participant. Whenever necessary, challenge should be designed so that each child will be assured of success. If a child attempts a task and has difficulty, help him or her only as much as is needed. Then give deserved positive feedback by isolating your praising commentary to what was actually accomplished. By praising his or her action in this manner, you give the child direct information he or she needs about his or her ability to perform. Praise of this nature which primarily describes, rather than evaluates, tells the child he or she is effective and worthy. It is additionally meaningful because it is proffered in the presence of others.

As each child undertakes his or her performance, encourage the other children to watch and "pull for him or her." When they become used to these success oriented Magic Circles, the children will begin to take pleasure in each others' accomplishments. An atmosphere of cooperation and congeniality gradually becomes more pronounced, especially when a success orientation is carried over into other activities at school.

Magic Circle Tasks in Unit Two

"I Can Act Like a Favorite Animal"

"I Can Paint a Picture and Tell You about It"

"I Can Play a Musical Instrument"

"I Can Sing a Song"

"I Can Make Something Out of Clay"

Magic Circle Task:
"I Can Act Like a Favorite Animal"

Purpose:

While peers observe, this Magic Circle formally enables each child to demonstrate his or her developing ability to create a dramatic representation of an animal in a simplified version of the game, "charades." As the activity proceeds, the children also have the opportunity to witness the dramatic representations of their peers. As each child succeeds, he or she is acknowledged for this accomplishment. The likely result in each one is feelings of increased confidence in his developing ability to act and enjoyment at this developing ability in his peers.

Introduce the task:

After reviewing the Magic Circle Promises say in your own words: *"We're going to have a lot of fun in our Magic Circle today. Our task is: 'I Can Act Like a Favorite Animal.' Each one of us will have a chance to show what good actors we are by acting like an animal we like. The rest of us will try and guess what animal you are acting out. Let me show you how we will do it."*

Staying within the circle, act like a favorite animal of your own. Do this by assuming a representative facial expression, body involvement and sounds. Ask the children to guess what it is. After they have guessed the right answer, tell the children how you felt about acting so well that they were able to guess correctly.

Involve the children:

Say: *"Let's close our eyes and think for a moment about a favorite animal to act out. When you have thought of your favorite animal look up and I will know you are ready to take a turn."*

As each child acts out his favorite animal, ask the other children to guess what it is. Allow the group to chorus their answers and the child actor to respond when someone guesses correctly. Acknowledge the child's ability to act: *"Super, (Doug), you certainly can act well!"* Then ask: *"How did you feel when you were acting out a (horse)?" "How do you feel now that you acted out your horse so well that (Janie) was able to tell what you were?"* (Simply accept it if the children copy each other. This is very common, especially at first.)

Lead a summary by asking:

1. *"What was everyone (were some of us) able to do in this Magic Circle?"*
2. *"What kinds of feelings did we have?"*

Guide the children to focus on the fact that all (or some) of them took a turn and did a fine job of acting like an animal. Talk about how some individuals had similar feelings about acting like animals and doing so well that others were able to guess what animal they were acting out. And others had different kinds of feelings. By your matter-of-fact manner, make it clear that it's okay for each person to feel as he or she does.

Conclude the Magic Circle:

Thank the children for joining in and cooperating to make the circle so enjoyable today.

Related Activity:

Warm the children up for this Magic Circle by singing "Old MacDonald Had a Farm." Divide the children into groups: cows, chickens, pigs, goats, horses, etc. After the first verse, point to the "cows" so all of the children will know the next line. Invite the "cows" to get up and act like cows while singing by themselves: "with a moo moo, here and a moo moo there; here a moo, there a moo; everywhere a moo moo...." Continue until all of the verses have been sung and each group has had a chance to act like an animal.

Magic Circle Task:

"I Can Paint a Picture and Tell You about It"

Purpose:

This Magic Circle formally enables children to demonstrate their developing abilities to paint and to talk about their paintings while their peers listen, and then to witness them do likewise. As each child succeeds, he is praised for his accomplishment. The likely result in each child is feelings of increased confidence in his developing talents and pleasure at the talents of others.

Materials needed:

Paints and large sheets of paper for each child.

Notes:

Prior to conducting this Magic Circle session, have the children paint pictures. Make sure the children understand that these paintings may be of real things, like animals, people and houses or designs with lots of shapes, lines, or colors. As the children paint their pictures, talk to them about their paintings to help prepare them for the Magic Circle.

Collect the paintings and write the children's names on them. As you conduct this Magic Circle, have the paintings on hand to give to the children as they share. (Make sure to paint your own too.)

During the Magic Circle, jot down on a note pad one sentence verbatim that each child says about his or her painting. Later, these statements can be used as captions for a display. (See "Related Activity" below.)

Introduce the task:

After reviewing the Magic Circle Promises and thanking the children for their attention, tell them in your own words: *"Today, our Magic Circle task is called: 'I Can Paint a Picture and Tell You about It.' We have already painted our pictures so in our circle we will have a chance to show them to each other and talk about them. I will go first so you can see how we will do this."*

Hold up the picture you have painted and tell the children about it briefly. For example: *"Here is my painting. It's a picture of my garden. Here are my roses and here are my berries. Can you guess what this is?* (The children respond.) *Right you are; it's a scarecrow! It scares away the birds. I had fun using many bright colors while painting this picture."*

Involve the children:

Ask: *"Now, who would like to show us your painting and tell us about it?"* As the children volunteer, hand them their pictures to show and talk about.

If a child experiences difficulty telling about her picture, help her by making positive comments and asking questions such as: *"What interesting shapes and colors! Tell us about this part here." "How did you feel when you were painting it?"* or *"How do you feel when you look at your painting now?"*

Continue this process, allowing each child who wishes to share, a chance to do so, acknowledging each child's efforts: *"That was very fine, Jay. You painted a design with so many bright colors! You also told us about it and how you felt when you did it. Thanks."* Collect the paintings so they won't distract the children while others are sharing.

Conduct a review (optional) by saying:

"Let's see how well we can remember. Some (or all) of us showed the picture we painted and told

about it. Who remembers (Jay's) painting and what he said about it? Raise your hand." Call on individual children to tell each other about their paintings and what they said about them.

As each one reviews to another, reinforce the child: *"How well you listened to (Jay). You remembered he said his painting was a design of some of his favorite colors. Now does anybody remember how he said he felt when he was painting his picture?"* Reinforce again those who remember specific feelings reported. Be sure each child who spoke during the session is reviewed to; it is important no one is left out of the review including yourself.

Lead a summary by asking:

1. *"What was everyone who shared today able to do?"*

2. *"Do you remember some of the feelings we said we had when we painted our pictures?"*

3. *"Is it okay for you to feel different than other people feel?*

As much as possible, in free-flowing discussion, allow the children to supply responses to these questions themselves. Affirm their understanding that all (or some) of them were able to paint a picture (realistic or abstract) and to tell about it. Emphasize that everyone has his or her own feelings and that's what makes us special and interesting to each other.

Conclude the session:

Thank the children for sharing their paintings and for making the circle so successful.

Related Activity:

Create a display of the children's paintings. If you have made notes of their remarks when they presented their paintings use them to create verbatim captions and place each one under the appropriate painting on the wall. Later, ask the children to view the display with you. Hold a discussion about how colorful and interesting it is. Focus on each painting and its caption. Read each one to the children and then ask them to read it with you in unison.

Magic Circle Task:

"I Can Play a Musical Instrument"

Purpose:

This Magic Circle formally enables each child to demonstrate his developing ability to play a musical instrument while his peers listen and observe, and then to witness them do likewise. Additionally, the children will all hear a recording of themselves playing their instruments. As the children succeed, they are individually acknowledged for their accomplishments. The likely result in each child is feelings of increased confidence in his or her developing talents and appreciation of the talents of others.

Note: Introduce musical instruments to the children before this Magic Circle so that they will have had some experience with them beforehand.

Materials needed:

A wide variety of preschool/kindergarten musical instruments such as drums, shakers, sandpaper blocks, whistles, castanets, triangle, bells, etc.; recording device.

Introduce the task:

After reviewing the Magic Circle Promises and thanking the children for their attention, tell them in your own words: *"Our Magic Circle task today is: 'I Can Play a Musical Instrument' Each one of us is going to get a chance to show how we can play one of our class instruments. Here is the musical instrument box. Let's look inside and see the instruments we will play."*

Show the children each instrument and demonstrate how to play it. Then continue: *"Each of you will have a chance to choose an instrument and play it. We will record you and play it back so you can hear yourself playing. Won't that be fun? After everyone who wants to has played an instrument we will put all our instruments together to form a band. We will record our band and listen to it too."*

Involve the children:

Ask: *"Who would like to come and pick an instrument out of the box and show us how you can play it?"* Allow each child to choose an instrument and demonstrate how she can play it as you record the performance. Acknowledge each child for playing the instrument so well.

After each performance, play back the recording, encouraging the children to share in the child's pleasure at hearing him- or herself playing the instrument. Allow the children to take their instruments back to their places in the circle and put them under their chairs for the grande finale.

When everyone who wishes to has taken a turn, tell the children: *"Now that each of you have played your instrument for us, we will form a band and play together. I will record us and then we will listen to the recording. Here is how we will do it. When I point to an instrument everyone who has that instrument will play it. When I point to two different instruments everyone who has those instruments will play them together. When I point to all the instruments at the same time we will all play our instruments together. When you are playing and I bring my hand up like this, play your instrument very loud. When I move my hand down like this, play it softly. Let's practice a little bit first."*

Lead a summary by asking:

1. *"What were we able to do?"*

2. *"What were some of the feelings we had when we played our instruments in front of the group?"*

3. *"How did you like hearing yourself play an instrument on the tape and when we played together in a band?"*

As much as possible, in free-flowing discussion, allow the children to supply responses to these questions themselves. Affirm their understanding that each child who participated played a musical instrument successfully. Emphasize the point that doing things well is important to everyone because it makes us feel good about ourselves.

Conclude the Magic Circle:

Thank the children for paying attention to each other and for making the circle a success.

Related Activity:

Make up a chant with the children reflecting who played what instrument during the Magic Circle. As you point to each child, the group chants about him and what he played. The chant could be punctuated by having each child play his instrument at designated intervals. For example:

"Johnnie plays the drum. Da dum, da dum, da dum!"

(Johnnie drums for 5 - 10 seconds.)

"Nicole plays the whistle. Ta weet, ta weet, ta weet!"

(Nicole blows into the whistle for 5 - 10 seconds.)

"Buddy plays the sandpaper blocks. Sca ratch, sca ratch, sca ratch!"

(Buddy moves sandpaper blocks for 5 - 10 seconds.)

Etc.

Practice the chant; then record it and play it back for everyone to hear and enjoy. Finally, hold a culminating discussion with the children about how the chant sounded and some of the feelings they had while they chanted, played instruments, and listened to the recording.

Magic Circle Task:

"I Can Sing a Song"

Purpose:

Children love to sing in groups, but seldom have a chance to sing alone for others and feel good about it. This Magic Circle formally enables each child to demonstrate his or her developing ability to sing and then hear a recording of herself singing. The children will also receive individual verbal recognition from others for this accomplishment. The likely result in each child is feelings of increased confidence in his or her developing ability to sing and pleasure at this developing ability in peers.

Materials needed:

Recording device.

Introduce the task:

After reviewing the Magic Circle Promises, tell them in your own words: *"Our Magic Circle task today is: 'I Can Sing A Song.' We will be singing songs together, but each of us will also have a chance to sing part of a song all by ourselves."*

Involve the children:

Ask the children to suggest some of their favorite songs to sing together. After they have sung two or three, have them sing "The Farmer in the Dell" or any other familiar song with a repetitive verse they can easily remember and sing on their own.

Turn on the recorder and then announce: *"Now each of you will have a chance to sing by yourself. I'll go first. Then if you want to be next raise your hand and if you are selected you can sing the next verse by yourself. Before we're done each one of us will get a chance to sing a verse alone. My verse will be 'The farmer takes a wife.' Then we need someone to volunteer for 'The farmer takes a child.' What else does the farmer take?"* Brainstorm all the possibilities for verses to this song (child, nurse, horse, cow, cat, dog, goat, hen, rooster, etc.). Then begin by singing the first verse, in unison, all the way through.

To assure the children a successful experience assist them by singing along very softly if needed. When each one finishes his verse, acknowledge his performance by saying something like: *"Wonderful (Tom). You sure can sing!"* Additionally, urge the other children to openly appreciate their classmates' performances.

After all of the children who wish to sing have sung, discuss how it felt to sing alone. Begin by telling the children how you liked singing by yourself. You could say something like this: *"That was fun! It felt a little strange, but nice to sing all by myself. How was it for you? Who would like to tell us how you felt singing for us all by yourself?"*

Finally, turn on the recorder and enjoy the recording together. If the children laugh, explain to the group that no one is being laughed at. It is very common for people to laugh at the strangeness of a familiar voice when they hear a recording of it because it sounds so different to them.

Lead a summary by asking:

1. *"What were we able to do in this Magic Circle today?"*
2. *"Do you remember some of the feelings we said we had about singing all by ourselves for the group?"*

Affirm their understanding that all of the children who volunteered to take a turn sang well all by themselves. Discuss the point that everyone enjoys doing something well and singing so well is a special way to make ourselves and others feel happy.

Conclude the Magic Circle:

Thank the children for doing such a fine job of singing and making the circle a success.

Related Activity:

Teach the children songs that can be sung in rounds such as Row, Row, Row Your Boat. Record their singing and play it back for their enjoyment.

Magic Circle Task:

"I Can Make Something Out of Clay"

Purpose:

This Magic Circle formally enables each child to demonstrate his or her developing ability to form and manipulate clay and then tell about what was sculpted while peers observe and listen, and then to witness them do likewise. As each child succeeds, he is acknowledged for his or her accomplishment. The likely result in each child is feelings of increased confidence in a developing ability to sculpt and appreciation for this developing ability in peers.

Note:

Because the intent of this Magic Circle is to provide each child with a successful experience, it is best not to use this session to introduce working with clay. Be sure the children have sculpted with some success beforehand.

Additional notes:

This Magic Circle includes time for creation and will therefore take longer than previous sessions.

During the session, jot down on a note pad what each child says his or her completed clay form is. Later, these statements can be used as markers for a display. (See "Related Activity" below.)

Materials needed:

An eight ounce piece of modeling clay or play doh for each child in the Magic Circle. (If these are different colors it will add interest.) Temporary labels to identify each child's completed clay form.

Introduce the task:

After reviewing the Magic Circle Promises and thanking the children for their attention, tell them in your own words: *"Today, our Magic Circle task is called: 'I Can Make Something Out of Clay.' And look what I've got here. Let me give each of you a piece of this clay. As soon as you get your piece, start to move it around in your hands. Today, each of us will make a creation out of this clay. Then, if you want to share, you can tell us what you made."*

As the children manipulate the clay, discuss with them how each time they use clay they get better at it. Discuss also how clay acts: Once it's been warmed up by the hands it's easy to move. Talk about how to pinch, pull, roll, and squeeze the clay, to form interesting shapes, maybe even shapes like animals or people. During this discussion, demonstrate some of these movements. For example, pull out four parts of your piece of clay to form legs for a four-legged animal. Then pull out a neck and head at one end and a tail at the other. Embellish with two pressed-on tiny balls for eyes and some pinched-out ears. (Reassure the children that it's okay not to make an animal; an interesting form will be just fine.)

When the children are finished, ask them to place their creations under their chairs. Tell them you'd like to start the sharing part of the Magic Circle. Take your turn first: *"Here is what I made out of clay. It is a frog. Here is his body; here are his legs. This is his head with big bulging eyes. And here is his mouth and curled-up tongue. It was hard to make because the tongue kept falling off. Now that it's finished I feel proud that I made it."*

Involve the children:

Ask: *"Now, who would like to show us your clay creation and tell us about it?"* As the children volunteer, assist them no more than necessary. If a child experiences difficulty, help her by making positive comments and asking open-ended questions such as: *"What a wonderful shape, (Sally)! Tell us about it." "How did you feel when you were making it?"* or *"How do you feel when you look at it now?"* Also invite the other children to encourage the child who is displaying her clay form and telling about it. Let them know they can join this child in feeling proud.

Continue this process, allowing each child who wishes to share, a chance to do so. As each one completes his remarks, point out how successful he was: *"Peter, you created such a fine dinosaur! You also told us about it and how you felt when you did it. Thanks."*

Collect each child's clay form as soon as he or she has shared so it won't be altered during the rest of the session. (Additionally, place an identification marker beside each child's creation so you will know who created each one. This information is necessary for the related activity described below.)

Conduct a review (optional) by saying:

"Let's see how well we can remember. Some (or all) of us showed the things we created out of clay and told about it. Who remembers (Sally's) creation and what she said about it? Raise your hand." Call on individual children to tell each other about their clay forms and what they said about them.

As each one reviews to another, reinforce the child: *"How well you listened to (Sally). You remembered she said her creation was a horse. Now does anybody remember how she said she felt when she was creating it?"* Reinforce again those who remember specific feelings reported. Be sure each person who shared during the session is reviewed to, including yourself.

Lead a summary by asking:

1. *"What was everyone able to do today?"*
2. *"Did everyone make the same thing out of clay? Is it okay to be different?"*
3. *"Do you remember some of the feelings we said we had when we made our creations out of clay?"*

As much as possible, in free-flowing discussion, allow the children to supply responses to these questions themselves. Affirm their understanding that all of them were able to create something out of clay and some (or all) of them told the group about their creations. Emphasize that everyone has his or her own likes, dislikes and feelings and that's what makes us special and interesting to each other.

Conclude the session:

Thank the children for their cooperation and for making this Magic Circle so successful.

Related Activity:

Place each child's completed sculpture on a display table. Put round markers cut from different colors of construction paper under each one. Write a statement on each marker identifying the item and its creator. For example:

This is Sally's horse.

This is Peter's dinosaur. Etc.

Later, ask the children to view the display with you. Hold a discussion about how colorful and interesting it is. Focus on each clay form and its statement. Read each one to the children and then ask them to read it with you aloud.

Unit III

Social Development and Responsibility Relating Responsibly with Others

This unit offers an initial, "hands-on" set of activities for children enabling them to directly experience effective interpersonal communication.

Relating positively with other people and behaving responsibly are challenges we all face. These are matters constantly at the forefront of all of our lives. Schools have long been charged with developing good citizenship and responsible social behavior in students. But the task of building socially responsible individuals is not an easy one. When schools have fallen short of this goal, it has not been from lack of concern, or even effort, but because they have lacked a structured, experiential means to this end.

Perhaps the most obvious characteristic of the Magic Circle is that it systematically offers children the opportunity to practice responsible behavior and effective communication skills with each other and with their teacher. Ineffective modes of communication are eliminated. This unit continues in that vein. Additionally, it offers specific tasks for the children to undertake which relate directly to key aspects of communicating in positive ways. These tasks relate to giving and receiving greetings, statements of appreciation, and compliments and responding to others' inquiries.

By participating in the activities in this unit the children are enabled to experience the rewards of effective communication and responsible behavior, both intrinsically and extrinsically. They may take pleasure in affecting others positively and may also appreciate being the recipients of effective communication directed toward them.

Magic Circle Tasks in Unit Three

"I Can Greet You"

"I Can Thank You for Doing Something I Liked"

"I Can Say Something Nice to You"

"I Can Tell You What I Like about Your Picture"

"I Can Show How I Answer the Door"

Magic Circle Task:

"I Can Greet You"

Purpose:

Acknowledging a person in a friendly way upon meeting, and being acknowledged in a similar manner, are fundamental to viable human relationships. In this Magic Circle, the children are able to practice giving and receiving friendly greetings and to talk about how these greetings affect them emotionally.

Introduce the task:

After reviewing the Magic Circle Promises and thanking the children for their attention, tell them in your own words: *"We're going to do something different in our Magic Circle today. Our task is: 'I Can Greet You.' Each one of us, who wishes to, will have a chance to greet another person in the circle by saying his, or her, name along with a greeting. Before we get started, let's talk about what a greeting is."*

Discuss the different ways one person can greet another, including: *"Hi!" "Hello there!" "How's it going?" "Nice to see you!"* Etc. Talk about how greetings can be accompanied with a wave, a pat on the back, a handshake, and even a hug. Tell the children: *"Today you will have a chance to greet someone in the circle by naming and greeting him, or her, in a way that feels good to you. I will go first and show you how we will do it."*

Select a child and ask him to leave the circle for a moment and then to return. Explain to the children that you are going to pretend that you have not seen this child yet today so when he returns you will greet him in a friendly way. After you have greeted the child, in a way that is comfortable for you, ask him: *"How did it make you feel when I greeted you, (Tommy)?"* (Listen to, and accept, his response.) Then tell the children how you felt. You might say something like this: *"I enjoyed greeting (Tommy). I noticed he smiled as soon as I did it and that gave me a good feeling."*

Involve the children:

Ask: *"Who would like to pick someone to greet?"* Select a child and ask who she would like to greet; then ask that child to leave and then come back to the circle. Give the first child the go-ahead, assisting with her greeting only if absolutely necessary. When both children have been reseated, ask them both how they felt beginning with the one who received the greeting. Reinforce the greeter: *"Very nice, (Robin). Your warm hello and wave to (Ricky) was enjoyable to watch."*

Then ask: *"Who else would like greet someone who has not been greeted yet?"* Continue until all of the children who wish to greet another have had a chance, but be sure all of the children receive a greeting, even if you deliver those greetings yourself.

Lead a summary by asking:

1. *"What did we do today in this Magic Circle?"*
2. *"What kinds of feelings did we have?"*

Guide the children to focus on the fact that all of them received a greeting and all (or some) of them greeted. Talk about how good it makes most people feel most of the time to be greeted. It makes us feel noticed and important. It also feels good to be the greeter because then we get to make someone else feel good.

Conclude the Magic Circle:

Thank the children for joining in and cooperating to make the circle so enjoyable today.

Related Activity:

In the days following this Magic Circle, be sure to model warm greetings to all of the children each day. Suggest that they remember to greet you, and each other, each day too. Frequently reinforce them for their friendly greetings.

Magic Circle Task:

"I Can Thank You for Doing Something I Liked"

Purpose:

Acknowledging and being thanked for one's positive behavior is a fundamental element in effective relationships. In this Magic Circle, the children are enabled to practice giving and receiving statements of thanks for their appreciated actions and to talk about how these statements affect them emotionally.

Introduce the task:

After reviewing the Magic Circle Promises, tell the children in your own words: *"Do you remember what we did in our last Magic Circle to make each other feel good? (The children respond.) That's right! We greeted each other! Today we're going to make each other feel good again. Our task is: 'I Can Thank You for Doing Something I Liked.' Each one of us, who wishes to, will have a chance to thank another child by saying his, or her, name and then thanking him for something he, or she, did that we felt good about. Then that person may say, 'You're welcome.'"*

Discuss some things the children have done that for which they could be thanked. Be sure to say at least one thing about each child. Then explain: *"Today you will have a chance to choose someone and thank him, or her, for doing something you really liked. First you say his, or her, name and then say, 'Thank you for....' I will go first and show you how we will do it."*

Tell the group: *"I want to thank (Amanda) for something she did this morning. (Amanda), thank you for picking up the apples I dropped and for putting them back in the basket when we were having our nutrition break. You were a big help."* Allow the child to say, *"You're welcome."* (Give a gentle reminder, if necessary.) Then ask the child: *"How did it make you feel when I thanked you, (Amanda)?"* (Listen to, and accept, the child's response.) Then tell the children how you felt. You might say something like this: *"I felt good about thanking (Amanda) because I really did appreciate it when she helped me with the apples this morning."*

Involve the children:

Ask: *"Who would like to pick someone to thank?"* Select a child and ask him who he would like to thank. Give the child selected the go-ahead, assisting him with his statement of appreciation only if absolutely necessary. After the child is finished, ask both children how they felt beginning with the one who received the thanks. Reinforce the child who delivered the thank you: *"Well done, (Donna). You remembered that (Shirley) played with you before school started this morning and you did a nice job of thanking her."*

Then ask: *"Who else would like to thank someone for doing something you liked, someone who has not been thanked yet?"* Continue in this manner until all of the children have had a chance, but be sure all of the children receive a statement of appreciation, even if you deliver those thanks yourself.

Lead a summary by asking:

1. *"What did we do today in this Magic Circle?"*
2. *"What kinds of feelings did we have?"*

Affirm the children's understanding that all of them received a thank you, and all (or some) of them thanked someone else. Talk about how good it makes us feel when we receive thanks for doing nice things. It makes us feel appreciated. It also feels good to the one who thanked the other because then we get to make someone else feel good.

Conclude the Magic Circle:

Thank the children for helping to make the Magic Circle such a success today.

Related Activity:

In the days following this Magic Circle, be sure to model showing your appreciation to the children for their positive and helpful actions by thanking them. Suggest that they remember to thank you and each other each day for doing things they like. Frequently reinforce them when they say thank you.

Magic Circle Task:

"I Can Say Something Nice to You"

Purpose:

This Magic Circle enables each child to practice giving and receiving a simple compliment, both important social skills. In the process the children may learn that they don't necessarily need to have "things" in order to have friends. Rather, friendship is more easily created and maintained when friends can sincerely express what they like about each other.

Introduce the task:

Tell the children in your own words: *"Let's start off our Magic Circle today by remembering what we did in our last two sessions. Does anyone remember?"* Discuss the greetings and thanks the children gave each other with them. Talk briefly about how these behaviors made them feel. Then explain: *"Today our Magic Circle will be similar, but a little bit different. The task is called: 'I Can Say Something Nice to You.' When someone says something nice to someone else we call it a 'compliment.' Let's all say that word.* (Repeat it in unison two or three times.) *In this Magic Circle each one of us will hear someone say something nice to us. And each of us will have a chance to pick someone and say something nice to him, or her. Then we will thank each other for the compliments we gave.*

"Before we begin, let's think of some nice things we could say to someone else." Brainstorm several meaningful compliments with the children, such as: *"You are fun to play with!" "I like your smile." "You look nice today." "I like you!"* Etc. Then remind the children that the person complimented might best respond by saying, *"Thank you."* Then tell the children: *"I will go first and show you how we will do it."*

Select a child and give him, or her, a sincere compliment. You could say something like this: *"I choose (Mae). (Mae), I like to hear you talk because you often say interesting things."* After you have complimented the child in a way that is comfortable for you, wait for her to say, *"Thank you."* (If the child doesn't, gently remind him, or her.) Then ask the child: *"How did it make you feel when I told you I like to hear you talk, (Mae)?"* (Listen to, and accept, the child's response.) Then tell the children how you felt about giving the compliment. You might say something like this: *"I enjoyed saying something nice to (Mae). It gave me a good feeling when she giggled and said thank you."*

Involve the children:

Ask: *"Who would like to pick someone to say something nice to?"* Select a child and ask him who he would like to compliment. Give the child the go-ahead, assisting him with his compliment only if absolutely necessary. After the compliment has been delivered and accepted, ask both children how they felt about it beginning with the one who received it. Reinforce the child who gave the compliment: *"Good for you, (Randy), you told (Janie) that you like her braids. That was a fine compliment."*

Then ask: *"Who else would like to say something nice to someone who has not received a compliment yet?"* Continue in this manner until all of the children who wish to deliver a compliment have had a chance, but be sure all of the children receive a compliment, even if you deliver those compliments yourself.

Lead a summary by asking:

1. *"What did we do today in this Magic Circle?"*

2. *"How does it make you feel to receive a compliment?"*

3. *"How does it make you feel to give a compliment?"*

Guide the children to focus on the fact that all of them received a compliment and all (or some) of them gave a compliment. Talk about how good it makes most people feel most of the time to be complimented. It makes us feel liked. It also feels good to be the one who gives a compliment because then we get to make someone else feel good.

Conclude the Magic Circle:

Thank the children for joining in and cooperating to make the circle so enjoyable today.

Prepare for the next Magic Circle: In the time between this and the next Magic Circle, carry out an art activity with the children. The objective is to obtain one painting, or drawing, from each child who will be participating in the next session. These pictures may be realistic or abstract designs. Write each child's name on the back of his picture.

Related Activity:

In the days following this Magic Circle, model giving sincere compliments to all of the children each day. Suggest to them that they remember to compliment you, and each other, whenever they honestly feel like it. Frequently reinforce them for their sincere attempts to be complimentary.

Magic Circle Task:
"I Can Tell You What I Like about Your Picture"

Purpose:
This Magic Circle enables each child another opportunity to practice giving and receiving compliments, this time relative to pictures they have painted, or drawn.

Materials needed:
A painting, or drawing created by each child with the child's name.

Introduce the task:
Tell the children in your own words: *"Do you remember what we did in our last Magic Circle? (The children respond.) Yes, indeed we said nice things to each other; we gave each other compliments."* Briefly discuss how the compliments made the children feel. Then say: *"Today we are going to get another chance to compliment each other. Our Magic Circle task is: 'I Can Tell You What I Like about Your Picture.' Remember the pictures we created to get ready for this Magic Circle? Well, here they are. We're going to look at each one and tell the artist what we like about his picture. Then we will thank each other for the compliments we gave each other."*

"Before we begin, let's think of some nice things we could say to someone about his picture." Brainstorm several compliments relative to art work with the children, such as: *"It is a cute picture!" "It's funny. I like to look at it." "You made some interesting lines and shapes." "I like the colors you used."* Etc. Then remind the children that the person complimented might best respond by saying, "Thank you." Then tell the children: *"Let me show you how we will do this."*

Involve the children:
Select a child's picture and say: *"This is (Mark's) painting. I know what I like about it. I really like this part here. It looks like a deep hole, kind of scary."* Then ask the children, *"What do you like about it? Raise your hand."* Call on individual children who wish to compliment the artist and encourage him to thank the group for their compliments. Then ask him: *"How did it make you feel when we told you all the things we like about your picture, (Mark)?* Proceed in this manner until all of the pictures have been viewed and the artists complimented by the group.

Lead a summary by asking:
1. *"What did we do in this Magic Circle?"*
2. *"What kinds of feelings did we have?"*

In free-flowing discussion allow the children to supply responses to these questions themselves. Affirm their understanding that all of them received several compliments about their pictures and all (or some) of them gave a compliment to someone else. Talk about how good it makes most people feel most of the time to receive compliments for something we have done. It makes us glad to know that other people like what we did. It also feels good to be the one who gives a compliment because then we get to make someone else feel good.

Conclude the Magic Circle:
Thank the children for helping to make the Magic Circle such a success today.

Related Activity:
Make a book of the children's pictures and place it where they can view it when they have free time. A good title for the book might be, "We Like Each Other's Pictures."

Magic Circle Task:

"I Can Show How I Answer the Door"

Purpose:
This Magic Circle enables the children to practice responding effectively to callers at the door whether grown-ups are at home or whether they are alone, or with other children only.

Materials needed:
Recording device.

Introduce the task:
Tell the children in your own words: *"Today our Magic Circle task is: 'I Can Show How I Answer the Door.' Each one of you is going to get two chances to show how you can answer the door. But first, let's talk about the most important thing we should do when we answer the door. We should be friendly to the person who is there, and talk in a nice way."*

Amuse the children with a little drama in which you pretend someone has knocked at your door and you respond in a rude manner: *"Knock, knock. ... Who's there? (snarling voice) I'm too busy! Go away."* Discuss how such behavior would probably make the person at the door feel. Then replay the scene responding in a friendly way and discuss how your friendliness would affect the person at the door.

Tell the children: *"Today we're going to do a lot of pretending. We will have a chance to practice being friendly to somebody at the door whether the person they came to see is at home or not. Let's start with times someone comes to the door and you are home all alone or with other children. There are no grown-ups at home. Should you open the door?"* At this point make sure the children understand that they should not open the door until they call out, *"Who's there?"* If they know the person to be a friend, or relative, they should open the door and, in a friendly way, ask the person in. **If they don't know the person they should not open the door at all, but say, *"My (mother) can't come to the door right now. Please come back later."*** Discuss with the children why they would not tell the person their (mother) is not at home nor open the door in instances of this nature. Point out, however, that they can still be friendly.

Involve the children:
Show the children that the imaginary door is in the middle of the circle. Then turn on the recorder and ask them: *"Who would like to try it first?"* Select a child and tell her to stand up and imagine that she is at home alone except for her sister who is seven years-old and someone she doesn't know knocks on the door. (You will pretend to be the stranger.) Make sure she understands she should not open the door. Then stand up and carry out the drama, assisting the child to respond correctly only as needed. At the completion of the drama reinforce the child: *"Well done, (Betty). You were smart not to open the door at all. You told me your Dad couldn't come to the door and asked me to come back. And you did it in a friendly way. Now who else would like to give it a try?"*

After about half of the children have had a turn, change the format by asking them to imagine that you are no longer a stranger, but yourself at the door. You have come to see the child's mother. Ask for the next volunteer and make sure he understands he should open the door and invite you in *because he knows that you are a friend*. Then carry out this drama. At its completion, reinforce the child.

Proceed in this manner until each child who wishes to has had a chance. Be sure each time a child takes a turn you remind him of the specific circumstances he is facing.

Next, as a group, consider the circumstance that grown-ups are at home when someone knocks at the door. Explain to the children: *"Someone knocks at the door. You are nearest so you go to it and open it because grown ups are there and you know you are safe. What do you say? (Hello.) If you know the person and he is a friend or relative, what should you do? (Invite him in, close the door and ask him who he wants to see.) If he is a stranger, what should you do? (Ask, "Who do you want to see?" Then close the door and go get the person in your family to come to the door.) Let's try answering the door in friendly ways when grown-ups are at home and you are not alone."*

Begin this second round of turn-taking by pretending the person at the door is a friend and the person he has come to see is at home. After about half of the children have responded to this situation ask them to imagine that the person at the door is a stranger. Then invite the other half of the children to respond to this second set of circumstances. Be sure to remind each child of the specific circumstances he is facing before he takes his turn. Record each of these dramas and reinforce each child after his turn for being friendly to the person at the door.

Lead a summary by asking:

1. *"What were we able to do?"*
2. *"When you answer the door in a friendly way how does it make the person at the door feel?"*

As much as possible, in free-flowing discussion, allow the children to supply responses to these questions themselves. Affirm their understanding that each child who participated responded well to the person at the door in a variety of circumstances. Emphasize that when they answer the door they can be friendly to the person there whether there are grown ups home or not, or whether the person the caller wants to see is at home or not. Being friendly makes the person at the door feel respected. It can also make us feel good when we know we treated another person well.

Conclude the Magic Circle:

Thank the children for paying such good attention and for doing such a good job of pretending in this Magic Circle.

Related Activity:

During an open play period after this Magic Circle, call the children individually to come and hear one, or both, of the recordings of themselves answering the door. Listen with each child to his recording. If necessary, help him perfect any weak spots in his response. Be sure to acknowledge each child for his efforts.

Unit IV

Self Awareness

Using and Enjoying Our Senses

This unit calls the children's attention to their senses and how they use them to perceive the world. By focusing directly on their senses the children are enabled to appreciate the gift of their senses and to begin to contemplate how they serve us. By participating in the Magic Circles and other activities in this unit, the children also are given the opportunity to discover that most human beings have all of the senses, but that each person experiences the world through his senses in his own individual manner. This provides the fundamental understanding for a developing sense of social awareness, empathy, and respect for differences.

In this unit we are moving the children from the physically involving Magic Circle Tasks to Magic Circle Topics which require only verbal participation. It is through this verbal sharing that children develop the confidence and repeatedly get the practice they need to develop their oral language abilities so they can effectively articulate their thoughts and feelings and needs.

Magic Circle Topics in Unit Four

"Something That Tastes Good"

"Something That Smells Good"

"Something I Enjoy Hearing"

"Something That Feels Good To My Fingers"

"Something I Enjoy Seeing"

Magic Circle Topic:

"Something that Tastes Good"

Purpose:

The children will be able to express feelings about tasting experiences and note similarities and differences in olfactory preferences. In the process they are enabled to gain an appreciation for the gift of taste.

Precede this Magic Circle with a tasting experience. This can be done while the children are in the circle or as a separate experience. Choose a number of foods that can be cut into small pieces. Pick foods having different flavors such as sweet, sour, tart, bland, spicy, etc. Pass each item around on a paper plate. After all the children have tasted the food ask: "How do you feel about the taste of this food? What kind of a taste does it have?" This process allows children to compare one taste with another. It also teaches them new vocabulary which describes flavors and allows them to talk about how they feel as they experience each taste.

Introduce the topic:

After reviewing the Magic Circle Promises tell the children in your own words: *"Today our Magic Circle topic is: 'Something that Tastes Good.' We are going to talk about things that taste good to us. One of the reasons we all enjoy eating is because most foods taste so good. I'd like to give you a chance to tell us about something that tastes especially good to you. It could be something you eat every day or it could be something that you only get to taste on special occasions or maybe have only tasted once. Perhaps it is something you or your parents buy at a store or it may be something that has to be made."*

"Let's close our eyes a few moments and use our memories. Let's think of some of our favorite foods and how they taste. What kinds of feelings did we have when we were eating them? Just think for a moment or two. When you are ready to tell us about it, open your eyes and look at me. Then I'll know you are ready to talk and listen."

Demonstrate that you are thinking about a favorite food and how it tastes by closing your eyes and concentrating for several seconds. If the children are not ready to speak, take a turn yourself. You could say something like this: *"The thing I am thinking about that tastes good is a tall glass of cold milk. It tastes especially good as it slides down my throat on a hot day. When I was little my mother used to call me and my friends in from play and give us milk and cookies. Milk tastes as good to me now as it did then."*

Involve the children:

Ask: *Who would like to tell about something that tastes especially good to you? Raise your hand when you are ready."*

As necessary, ask open-ended questions to individual children as they share, but do so sparingly: *"Tell us how you feel, (Howie) when you take the first bite of pizza? What part of the pizza tastes best to you? The cheese, crust, meat, etc.?"*

Since describing tastes may be a new experience for the children be patient with their efforts. Only give minimal assistance with their descriptions and be sure to demonstrate an accepting attitude about their explanations.

Lead a summary by asking:

1. *"Do the same things always taste good to everyone?*
2. *"What things did people like the taste of that were the same?*
3. *"What things did people like the taste of that were different? Is it okay to be different from other people?"*

As much as possible, in free-flowing discussion, allow the children to supply responses to these questions themselves. Guide them to focus on the fact that some people have similar tastes.

(Billy and Mary both like ice cream cones.) Also emphasize that people are frequently different from one another in their tastes. (Beth likes the sour taste of dill pickles. Ruth likes spicy chili-dogs.) Stress that these differences are acceptable and even desirable because they make us interesting to one another.

Conclude the Magic Circle:

End the circle by thanking the children for cooperating and making the circle a success.

Related Activity:

Follow up the Magic Circle by passing around a mixed plate of food and asking each child close his eyes and, after selecting a piece, guessing by its feel, smell and taste, what it is. (If the child guesses wrong give hints.)

Magic Circle Topic:
"Something that Smells Good"

Purpose:

The children will be able to express feelings about olfactory experiences and note similarities and differences in olfactory preferences in this Magic Circle. In the process they are enabled to gain an appreciation for their ability to smell.

Precede this Magic Circle with a smelling experience. This can be done while the children are in the circle or as a separate activity. Baby food jars wrapped in masking tape with holes punched in the lids to hide their contents work well for this experience. Choose a number of liquids and/or solids having a variety of scents and aromas, being sure that none of these items is harmful to the eyes or skin. You can make this a "matching smells" activity by having two of each kind of scent. Mix up the jars and have the children find the two that smell alike. Encourage the children to identify the contents of each jar as best they can and to describe the scent or aroma. Ask them also how they feel about each smell. This process allows them to compare smells and to learn new vocabulary describing scents and aromas. It also allows them to identify their affective reactions to each scent and aroma.

After each set of jars is discussed you can tell the children what they contain if they have not guessed correctly. Then unscrew the lids and show them what is inside each jar.

Introduce the topic:

After reviewing the Magic Circle Promises, tell they children in your own words: *"Today our Magic Circle topic is: 'Something that Smells Good.' We are going to talk about things that smell good to us. For sure, one of the things that all of us enjoys is smelling good things. One of the reasons we all enjoy eating food is because many foods smell so good. Many things that are not food smell good too. I'd like to give you a chance to tell us about some food or any other thing that smells especially good to you. It could be a treat your mother fixes for you to eat that smells so good when it's cooking. Or it could be a scent or aroma you smell on your way to school or when you are shopping with your mother."*

"Let's close our eyes a few moments and use our memories. Let's think of some of our favorite foods and other things that smell good to us. What kinds of feelings did we have when we were smelling them? Just think for a moment or two. When you are ready to tell us about it, open your eyes and look at me. Then I'll know you are ready to talk and listen."

Demonstrate that you are thinking about a favorite item and how it smells by closing your eyes and concentrating for several seconds. If the children are not ready to speak, take a turn yourself. You could say something like this: *"The thing I am thinking about that smells so good to me is fresh baked bread. It smells so very good when it is just hot from the oven. Just smelling it always makes me happy and hungry at the same time."*

Involve the children:

Ask: *"Who would like to tell about something that smells especially good to you? Raise your hand when you are ready."*

As necessary, ask open-ended questions to individual children as they share, but do so sparingly: *"Tell us how you feel, (Carolyn) when you take the first smell of the rose blossom? Do different roses have different scents or aromas?"*

Since describing scents and aromas may be a new experience for the children, be patient with their efforts. Only give minimal assistance with their descriptions and be sure to demonstrate an accepting attitude about their explanations.

Lead a summary by asking:

1. *"Do the same things always smell good to everyone?"*
2. *"What things did people like the smell of that were the same?"*
3. *"What things did people like the smell of that were different? Is it okay to be different from other people?"*

Guide the children to focus on the fact that some people like similar scents or aromas. (Carolyn and John both like the smell of roses.) Also emphasize that people are sometimes different from one another regarding what smells good to them. (Brent likes the smell of gasoline. Karen likes the smell of fresh paint.) Stress that these differences are acceptable and even desirable because they make us interesting to one another.

Conclude the Magic Circle: Thank the children for cooperating with you to make this Magic Circle a success.

Related Activities

Involve the children in other smelling experiences:

Take a class walk and discuss the different noticeable scents/aromas in the air.

Introduce the children to a variety of scratch and sniff stickers.

Read books about scents/aromas and about the olfactory sensory system and how it works.

Sing the Smell Song:

If you like to smell a ____, raise your hand.

If you like to smell a ____, raise your hand.

If you like to smell a ____ .

If you like to smell a ____ .

If you like to smell a ____ , raise your hand!

As this song is sung point to a child in the circle who then fills in the blank word to the verse. The children will come up with "skunk" and other delightful variations.

Magic Circle Topic:
"Something I Enjoy Hearing"

Purpose:

The children will be able to express feelings about auditory experiences and note similarities and differences in auditory preferences. In the process they are enabled to gain an appreciation for the gift of hearing.

Precede this Magic Circle with a listening experience. This can be done as a circle experience or as a separate activity. Suggest to the children: "Let's all close our eyes and be very quiet for a moment. Listen to the different sounds in the room and outside our room. When you hear a sound that is different and you would like to tell us about it, open your eyes, look up and I will know you are ready to tell us about what you have heard." As the children share, praise them for being such good listeners to sounds around them and to each other as they speak. Discuss the fact that there are many sounds around us we don't hear unless it is very quiet or unless we are especially listening for them.

Introduce the topic:

Tell the children in your own words: *"Today our Magic Circle topic is: 'Something I Enjoy Hearing.' We are going to talk about things we enjoy hearing. Hearing is one of our senses that we use all the time. We are surrounded by sounds, so many that we don't even pay attention to many of them. Some sounds are harsh and unpleasant to our ears. Some sounds feel good just like some things taste good and smell good. You will have a chance in this Magic Circle to tell about something that sounds especially good to you. It could be something you listen to in your room, or house. It could be something you hear at school or when you are outdoors. It could be something you hear everyday or it could be something that you don't hear very often or have only heard once or twice."*

"Let's close our eyes for a few moments and use our memories. Let's think of sounds we enjoy hearing very much. What kinds of feelings do we have when we are listening to a favorite sound? Just think for a moment or two. When you are ready to tell us about one of your favorite sounds, open your eyes and look at me. Then I'll know you are ready to talk and listen."

Demonstrate that you are thinking about something you enjoy hearing and how it sounds by closing your eyes and concentrating for several seconds. If the children are not ready to speak, take a turn yourself: *"The thing I enjoy hearing most is the sound of water in a fountain. It always makes me feel very restful and peaceful inside. Sometimes it makes me feel playful like I want to splash in the water and perhaps splash someone else who is nearby. The splashing sound makes me feel happy and at peace."*

Involve the children:

Ask: *"Who would like to tell about something you especially enjoy hearing? Raise your hand when you are ready."*

As necessary, ask open-ended questions to individual children as they share: *"Tell us how you feel, (Bobby,) when you hear the sound of your mother's voice reading to you? Is the sound of her voice different when she is reading to you than when she is calling you in or asking you to get something for her? How is it different?"*

Since describing sounds they enjoy hearing may be a new experience for the children be patient with their efforts. Only give minimal assistance with their descriptions and be sure to demonstrate an accepting attitude about their explanations.

Lead a summary by asking:

1. *"Is it good to be able to hear?"*
2. *"Does everyone enjoy hearing the same thing?"*
3. *"Is it okay if someone likes a sound no one else likes?"*

As much as possible, in free-flowing discussion, allow the children to supply responses to these questions themselves. Guide them to focus on how fortunate we are to be able to hear. Also emphasize the fact that some people enjoy hearing similar sounds. (Bobby and Grace both like being read to by their mothers.) But people are frequently different from one another in what they enjoy hearing. (I like the sound of water in a fountain. Bill likes to listen to his kitty purr when her pats her.) Stress that these differences are acceptable and even desirable because they make us interesting to one another.

Conclude the Magic Circle:

Thank the children for sharing and listening and for making the circle such a success.

Related Activities:

Play a variety of musical instruments and discussing how each one works to produce its particular sound.

Ask the children to close their eyes and listen carefully. Produce a sound with an instrument and ask them to raise their hands if they want to guess which instrument you used. Next, invite a child to produce the sounds while the other children close their eyes.

Ask the children to close their eyes while you walk noiselessly around the room. Make a sound and ask them to point to the direction they believe the sound came from. Then tell the children to open their eyes to test their perception. Next, invite a child to produce these sounds and tell the other children to open their eyes after they have pointed.

Magic Circle Topic:

"Something that Feels Good to My Fingers"

Purpose:

The children will be able to express feelings about tactile experiences and note similarities and differences in tactile preferences. In the process they are enabled to gain an appreciation for the gift of touch.

Precede this Magic Circle with a tactile experience. Distribute a number of items with a variety of textures around the circle for the children to touch. Tell them: "I am passing around some things that feel different to our touch. Let's name each one as we touch it. Who would like to tell how you feel when you are touching this first item?" Ask the children to categorize items that feel similarly (smooth or rough, soft or hard, etc.).

Introduce the topic:

Tell the children in your own words: *"Today our Magic Circle topic is: 'Something that Feels Good to My Fingers.' We are going to talk about things that feel good to our touch. Not everything feels good when we touch it. Some things are too hot, too cold, rough or sharp. These things are uncomfortable to us when we touch them. We learn when we are very young which things not to touch. But many things are okay to touch and some things feel very good to our fingers. I'd like to give you a chance to tell us about something that feels especially good to you when you touch it. It could be something you carry in your pocket like a rabbit's foot or a special rubbing stone. It could be something alive like a kitten or puppy. It could be something you touch every day or something you only get to touch on special occasions."*

"Let's close our eyes a few moments and use our memories. Let's think of something that feels so good when we touch it with our fingers. Just think for a moment or two. When you are ready to tell us about something that feels good when you touch it, open your eyes and look at me. Then I'll know you are ready to talk and listen."

Demonstrate that you are thinking about something you enjoy touching by closing your eyes and concentrating for several seconds. If the children are not ready to speak, take a turn yourself. You could say something like this: *"The thing I am thinking about that feels good when I touch it is moss growing on a tree or along a river bank or stream. I like to run my fingers back and forth across it. It feels so soft to my touch."*

Involve the children:

Ask: *"Who would like to tell about something that feels especially good when you touch or feel it? Raise your hand when you are ready."*

As necessary, ask open-ended questions to individual children as they share, but do so sparingly: *"Tell us how you feel, (Patricia), when you are petting your cat. Why does it feel so good to your hands and fingers?"*

Since describing tactile sensations may be a new experience for the children, be patient with their efforts. Only give minimal assistance with their descriptions and be sure to demonstrate an accepting attitude about their explanations.

Conduct a review (optional) by saying:

"Let's see how well we listened to each other. We told about many things that feel good to us when we touch them. Who can remember what (Patricia) told us? What was it she enjoys touching? Raise your hand if you want to tell her."

Call on the children to tell each other what they heard each other say, being sure each child who spoke is reviewed to. Reinforce the children: *"How well you listened to (Patricia). You heard her tell us how good it feels when she is rubbing the fur on her cat. Do you remember how she said she felt when she is petting it?"* Reinforce again those who remember specific positive feelings reported.

Lead a summary by asking:

1. *"Is it good to be able to feel things with our fingers?"*
2. *"Does everyone like to touch the same things?"*
3. *"What things did people like to touch that were different? Is it okay to be different from other people?"*

As much as possible, in free-flowing discussion, allow the children to supply responses to these questions themselves. Guide them to discuss how helpful and satisfying it is to be able to feel things with our fingers. Focus also on the fact that some people like the feel of the same things. (Patricia and Bill both like the feel of touching their pets.) Additionally, emphasize that people are frequently different from one another in what feels good to their touch. (Seth likes the feel of sand running through his fingers. Terri likes to feel the fishes' scales when her Mom or Dad catch a fish.) Stress that these differences are acceptable and even desirable because they make us interesting to one another.

Conclude the Magic Circle.

Thank the children for their cooperation in making the circle such a success.

Related Activities:

Take the children for a walk around the classroom and suggest they feel as many different surfaces as possible (wood, metal, cloth, etc.). Then bring them back to the circle to talk about what they experienced.

Take the children for a walk around the playground or neighborhood giving them the chance to have as many different tactile experiences as possible. Follow up with a circle discussion.

Magic Circle Topic:

"Something I Enjoy Seeing"

Purpose:

The children will be able to express feelings about visual experiences and note similarities and differences in visual preferences. In the process they are enabled to gain an appreciation for the gift of sight.

Introduce the topic:

Tell the children in your own words: *"Today our Magic Circle topic is: 'Something I Enjoy Seeing.' We are going to talk about things we like to look at. It is so good to enjoy all the beautiful and unusual sights around us. We are constantly using our eyes to bring us happiness. I'd like to give you a chance to tell us about something you enjoy looking at. Perhaps it is something you enjoy looking at at home. Maybe it is something in the classroom or outdoors."*

"Let's close our eyes a few moments and use our memories. Think of one special thing you like to look at. What kinds of feelings do you have when you are looking at it? When you are ready to tell us about something you like to look at, open your eyes and look up. Then I'll know you are ready to talk and listen."

Demonstrate that you are thinking about something you enjoy seeing by closing your eyes and concentrating for several seconds. If the children are not ready to speak, take a turn yourself. You could say something like: *"The thing I am thinking about that I like to see is all your smiling faces when you come into the classroom. It makes me feel warm inside when I see your bright faces looking at me. I know we will have a good time learning and having fun together."*

Involve the children:

Ask: *"Who would like to tell about something you enjoy seeing or looking at? Raise your hand when you are ready."*

Ask open-ended questions as the children share: *"Tell us how you feel, (Jeffrey), when you look at your collection of rocks? Are there some rocks you enjoy looking at more than others? Why do you enjoy looking at them more?"*

Since talking about the enjoyment of visual experiences may be new for the children, be patient with their efforts. Give minimal assistance with their descriptions and demonstrate an accepting attitude.

Lead a summary by asking:

1. *"Is it good that we can see?"*
2. *"Do we all enjoy looking at the same things?"*
3. *"What things did people like to see that were different? Is it okay for us to enjoy looking at different things?"*

Allow the children to supply responses to these questions themselves. Guide them to acknowledge how fortunate we are to be able to see. Focus also on the fact that some people have similar things they enjoy looking at. Also emphasize that people are frequently different from one another in what they like to look at. Stress that these differences are acceptable and even desirable because they make us interesting to one another.

Conclude the Magic Circle:

Thank the children for sharing and listening and for making the circle a success.

Related Activity:

Show the children photographs of different settings and seasons, including mountains, beaches, deserts in summer, fall, winter and spring. For each photograph ask the children: *"What do you see?"* Talk about how useful and wonderful it is to be able to see.

Unit V

Self Management

Showing What We're Learning

Designed to help children develop self-efficacy and celebrate their developing knowledge and skills, this unit offers six Magic Circle sessions having "success tasks." The purpose of these success tasks is two-fold. First, they assure each child a successful experience with a chance to talk about the good feelings that success brings. Second, the success tasks serve as a vehicle to give each child deserved, positive feedback immediately after his successful performance. This is an important time to receive such feedback because witnesses are present.

Since the self-esteem of each child is of prime importance, this unit should not be offered until you are certain the children will be able to meet each task successfully. Additionally, challenge should always be adjusted if needed during a session so each child is assured of success. If a child attempts a task and has difficulty, help him only as much as is necessary. Then isolate your praising commentary to what was actually accomplished. By praising his action in this manner, you give the child direct information he needs about his ability to manipulate the environment. Praise of this nature which describes, rather than evaluates, tells the child that he is effective and worthy.

As each child undertakes his performance, encourage the other children to watch and "pull for him." When they become used to these success oriented Magic Circles the children will begin to take pleasure in each other's accomplishments. An atmosphere of cooperation and congeniality gradually becomes more pronounced in the general learning environment, especially when a success orientation is carried over into other classroom activities.

Magic Circle Tasks in Unit Five

"I Can Show You Where Things are Kept"

"I Can Use Things"

"I Know Some Color Names"

"I Can Sort Things into Groups"

"I Know Some Letters of the Alphabet"

"I Know Some Numbers"

Magic Circle Task:
"I Can Show You Where Things are Kept"

Purpose:

This Magic Circle formally enables each child to demonstrate his developing ability to use his memory while his peers observe and then to witness them do likewise. As each child succeeds, he is praised for his accomplishment. The likely result in each child are feelings of increased confidence in his developing abilities and respect for the accomplishments of others.

Materials needed:

Prominent items from the classroom placed in a box with a lid. The number of these items should be double the number of children in the Magic Circle plus one.

Introduce the task:

After reviewing the Magic Circle Promises and thanking the children for their attention, tell them in your own words: *"Our Magic Circle task today is: 'I Can Show You Where Things are Kept.' Each one of you is going to get a chance to show that you know where we keep things in our classroom. Let me go first and I'll show you how we will do it."*

Present the box to the children and open the lid. Then reach in and pull out an item. You might say: *"Ah! Here's a (block). I know where it goes. We keep it in (the block basket with the other blocks). I'm going to take it over there right now and put it where it is kept."* Place the item where it belongs and then return to the circle.

Involve the children:

Ask: *"Now, who would like to choose one of the things in the box and put it where it is kept?"* Call on a volunteer and when the child correctly deposits the item in its proper place and returns to the circle, reinforce him: *"Good for you, (Joe). You knew where the ball is kept."*

Continue this process until all the children in the circle have had a chance to place an item from the box in its proper place in the classroom. As each child succeeds, encourage the other children to join him in feeling pride in himself. Occasionally ask the child who succeeded: *"How does it feel to do this right?"*

If the task goes quickly and the children enjoy it, give them another round, but vary the challenge by selecting an item from the box yourself and asking, *"Who can place this (drum) where it is kept?"* Each time a child succeeds make a statement to her reflecting her ability to remember where objects belong: *"That's very good, (Sara). You certainly do remember where things are kept!"*

Lead a summary by asking:

1. *"What was everyone able to do?"*
2. *"Why is it good for us to know where things are kept?"*

Affirm the children's understanding that each child knows where many things are kept. Bring out the point that we live happier lives when we can remember where things are kept and we make it a point to keep them there when we aren't using them.

Conclude the Magic Circle:

Thank the children for cooperating so well in making the circle a success.

Related Activity:

Surprise the children by sprinkling some trash on the floor for them to find when they enter from a recess. Ask them: *"Where is trash kept?"* Thank the children as they pick up the trash and place it in the wastepaper basket. At the end of each class session ask this same question, allowing the children to tidy up their classroom before leaving it.

Magic Circle Task:

"I Can Use Things"

Purpose:

This Magic Circle formally enables each child to demonstrate his developing ability to use things while his peers observe and then to witness them do likewise. As each child succeeds he is praised for his accomplishment. The likely result in each child are feelings of increased confidence in his developing abilities and pleasure at the accomplishments of others.

Materials needed:

Frequently used classroom and home items placed in a box with a lid. These items should be things the children have already learned to use, such as classroom musical instruments, a tooth brush, a crayon, a clothes hanger, etc. There should be one item for each child in the Magic Circle plus one.

Introduce the task:

Tell the children in your own words: *"Our Magic Circle task today is: 'I Can Use Things.' Each one of you is going to get a chance to show us that you know how to use something. It's going to be fun. Let me go first and I'll show you how we will do it."*

Take out the box and open the lid. Then reach in and pull out an item. You might say: *"Well, look here. I've got a book. I know how to use a book. I start by looking at the cover and opening it to the first page. Then I turn the pages like this, in this direction, and I look at the pictures on each page. If there's writing I read it. I go all the way through and look at each page including the back cover. I never start with a book at the back. I never tear it and I handle it with care."*

Involve the children:

Place the book to the side and then ask the children: *"Who would like to choose something from inside the box and show and tell us how you use it."* Call on a volunteer, helping him as needed to describe how he uses the item he has chosen. As each child completes his turn, reinforce him: *"Nice job, (Javier)! You certainly do know how to use a fork!"*

Continue this process until all the children in the circle have had a chance to show and tell the others how the item of his choice is used. As each one succeeds, encourage the other children to join him in feeling pride in himself. Occasionally ask the child who succeeded: *"How does it feel to know how to use things?"*

Lead a summary by asking:

1. *"What was everyone able to do?"*
2. *"How did we feel about being able to use things?"*

Affirm the children's understanding that each child knows how to use things. Emphasize the point that learning how to use, and do, things is good for us. As each day goes by we will continue learning and growing. And it's okay to be proud of ourselves for learning so well.

Conclude the Magic Circle:

Thank the children for cooperating so well in making the circle a success.

Related Activity:

Ask the children to draw a picture of themselves using something. After posting their completed art work on a bulletin board focus on each picture as a group. Ask each child to talk about his picture. As the children speak write down one sentence verbatim each one says. Later, make captions from these statements and place the appropriate one under each child's picture. The next day, refocus the children's attention on the display and read each caption to the children. Then ask them to read each one with you aloud.

Magic Circle Task:

"I Know Some Color Names"

Note:
Be sure that each child who participates in the Magic Circle knows the names of at least two colors.

Purpose:
This circle session formally enables each child to demonstrate his developing knowledge while his peers observe and then to witness them do likewise. As each child succeeds he is praised for his accomplishment. The likely result in each child are feelings of increased confidence in his developing abilities and appreciation for the accomplishments of others.

Materials needed:
5" x 5" pieces of construction paper in the primary colors (red, yellow and blue), secondary colors (green, orange and purple) and black and white; or any other collection of identically shaped objects in these colors.

Introduce the task:
Tell the children in your own words: *"Our Magic Circle task today is: 'I Know Some Color Names.' Each one of you is going to get a chance to show that you know some of the names of the colors. First, let's look at some of the colors and review their names."*

Present the three cards with the primary colors, red, yellow and blue, one at a time and ask the children to say their names with you as you present each one. Then say the names of all three colors in unison twice.

Involve the children:
Explain: *"Now, I will say the name of one of the colors and one of you will come up and point to it. Are you ready? Who would like to come up and point to the color yellow?"* Select a child who volunteers. If she experiences difficulty give her hints so that she may be successful, then say: *"Good for you, (Marcia), you know the color yellow."*

Continue this process until all the children in the circle have had a chance to come up and point to a color card. As each child succeeds, encourage the other children to join him in feeling pride in himself. Occasionally ask the child who succeeded: *"How does it make you feel to get it right?"*

If the task goes quickly and the children enjoy it give them another round with the secondary colors: green, orange and purple, and black and white. Repeat the same process of saying their names as a group and allowing the children to volunteer after you have named the color.

If the children have learned the color names well, you may introduce this more challenging variation: *"Now, who would like to point to a color I'm going to name without knowing which color it will be?"* Each time a child succeeds make a statement to him reflecting his ability to identify the correct color: *"Yes, indeed, (Davey), you pointed to the color I named. You certainly can learn the names of the colors!"*

Lead a summary by asking:
1. *"What was everyone able to do?"*
2. *"How did we feel about being able to point to the correct color?"*

As much as possible, in free-flowing discussion, allow the children to supply responses to these questions themselves. Affirm their understanding that each child knows many color names. The important point to emphasize is how good it feels to learn and that every day gives each one of us a chance to learn more about all sorts of things.

Conclude the Magic Circle:

Thank the children for cooperating so well to make the circle a success.

Related Activity:

Take a walk around the classroom with the children and point to various objects of one primary or secondary color, including black and white. You may also point to articles of clothing you and the children are wearing. (Multicolored objects and objects of subtle color are undesirable because they lead to confusion.)

As you point to each object allow the children to chorus its name. Each time you hear a correct response from the group reinforce them: *"That's right, it's purple! Good for you!"* When you end the activity reinforce the group: *"Great job! All of you are learning the names of the colors so well!"*

Magic Circle Task:
"I Can Sort Things into Groups"

Note:
Be sure that each child who participates in this session can make simple classifications of objects.

Purpose:
This Magic Circle formally enables each child to demonstrate her developing skills in the realm of classification while her peers observe, and then to witness them do likewise. As each child succeeds she is praised for her accomplishment. The likely result in each child are feelings of increased confidence in his developing abilities and pleasure at the accomplishments of others.

Materials needed:
Three bags, each with an assortment of objects. Bag 1 should contain items classifiable only into two categories (such as: a few pencils and a few pennies). Bags 2 and 3 should each contain a different assortment of items which could be classified in a variety of ways. For example, Bag 2 might contain: a few blue plastic dishes; a few metal hair barrettes, red, yellow and blue; a red plastic comb and brush set; a few nickels; a few metal spoons; a few crayons, red, yellow, blue, green, orange and purple; a few ball point pens; a few paper napkins; and a few yellow pencils.

These items belong to several categories or classes, as follows: (1) things we use at the table; (2) things used for the hair; (3) things we can use to write or draw a picture with; (4) round things; (5) long things, (6) plastic things, (7) metal things, (8) red things, (9) blue things, (10) yellow things, etc. (Note that one item may belong to several different classifications at the same time.)

Introduce the task:
Tell the children in your own words: *"Our Magic Circle task today is: 'I Can Sort Things into Groups.' Each one of you is going to get a chance to show how you can put things that belong with each other into groups. These things belong with each other because they are alike in some way. Let me show you what I mean."*

Present bag 1 and remove one of the forks and one of the pennies. Place each on the floor in front of you.

Involve the children:
Pull out another fork or penny and ask: *"Where should I put this?"* Continue, in this manner until all of the forks and pennies have been properly grouped, being sure to reinforce the children each time they make a correct response.

Next present bag 2 and remove all of the contents. Tell the children: *"Wow! Look at all of these things! Let's sort and group them. Here's how we'll do it. I will say a way to sort out some of these things and if you think you can do it raise your hand. Okay, who thinks you can find all the red things and put them in a group?"* As each child responds to the way you suggest a subgroup of items could be grouped, reinforce her: *"Terrific, (Donna), you sorted all of the round things into a group. You can do a good job of sorting!"* Be sure to discuss with the children how several things can belong to more than one group, according to color, shape, construction and purpose for which it is used, etc.

Continue this process until all the children in the circle have had a chance to sort the items into a group. As each child succeeds, encourage the other children to join him in taking pride in his accomplishment.

If the task goes quickly and the children enjoy it, offer this variation: present Bag 3 and its contents. Then ask, *"Who sees one way to sort out some of the things in this bag?"* As the children volunteer, ask them to explain why they are sorting them as such, helping them as necessary with their verbal explanations. (Be ready to discover that the children will find ways to sort the items you haven't thought of.) Be sure to reinforce each child for his performance, occasionally ask: *"How does it feel to know you can do this?"*

Lead a summary by asking:

1. *"What was everyone able to do?"*
2. *"Why is it good that we know how to sort things into groups?"*

As much as possible, in free-flowing discussion, allow the children to supply responses to these questions themselves. Affirm their understanding that each child was able to sort things into groups. Help the children understand that now they can sort many different things into groups anytime they want to. Point out that being able to do this is important because it makes our lives more understandable and orderly. It is an ability they will use all their lives in many ways.

Conclude the Magic Circle:

Thank the children for cooperating so well to make the circle a success.

Related Activity:

Ask the children to sort the things in their desks, cubbies, and/or backpacks and then to put everything back in this new organized and neat way.

Magic Circle Task:

"I Know Some Letters of the Alphabet"

Note:
Be sure that each child who participates in this session knows at least two letters of the alphabet.

Purpose:
This Magic Circle formally enables each child to demonstrate his developing knowledge of letters while his peers observe and then to witness them do likewise. As each child succeeds he is praised for his accomplishment. The likely result in each child are feelings of increased confidence in his developing abilities and pleasure at the accomplishments of others.

Materials needed:
Chart paper and a marker.

Introduce the task:
Tell the children in your own words: *"Our Magic Circle Task today is: 'I Know Some Letters of the Alphabet.' Each one of you is going to get a chance to show that you know some of the letters in the alphabet. We will do it in a way that's fun, but first let's review some of the letters."* Present the first five letters of the alphabet in capital form, one at a time, saying its name with the children as you write or display it.

Involve the children:
Explain: *"Now I will name of one of the letters and you can come up and point to it. Are you ready? Who would like to come up and point to the letter B?"* Select a child who volunteers. If he experiences difficulty give him hints so that he may be successful, then say: *"That's great (Bernardo), you know the letter B."*

Continue until all the children have had a chance to point to a letter. Occasionally ask the child who succeeded: *"How does it make you feel to get it right?"*

If the task goes quickly and the children enjoy it, give them another round with the next five letters of the alphabet, repeating the same process. The process may be continued until you have gone through the entire alphabet.

If the children have learned the letters well you may introduce this more challenging variation: *"Now, who would like to point to a letter I'm going to name without knowing which letter it will be?"* Each time a child succeeds make a statement to him reflecting his ability to identify the correct letter: *"Good for you (Annie), you pointed to the letter I named! You can learn the letters of the alphabet!"*

Lead a summary by asking:
1. *"What was everyone able to do?"*
2. *"How did we feel about being able to point to the correct letter?"*

In free-flowing discussion, allow the children to supply responses to these questions themselves. Affirm their understanding that each child knows many letters of the alphabet. The important point to emphasize is how good it feels to learn and that every day gives each one of us a chance to learn more about all sorts of things.

Conclude the Magic Circle:
Thank the children for cooperating so well to make the circle a success.

Related Activity:
Instead of teaching the children the traditional alphabet chant ("A is for Apple; B is for Bell,") create one with the children's help using their names. For examples: A is for Annie. B is for Bill. C is for Carol. D is for David. Etc.

Magic Circle Task:

"I Know Some Numbers"

Note:
Be sure that each child who participates in this Magic Circle knows the names of at least two numerals.

Purpose:
This circle session enables each child to demonstrate his developing knowledge of numbers while his peers observe and then to witness them do likewise. As each child succeeds he is praised for his accomplishment. The likely result in each child are feelings of increased confidence in his developing abilities and pleasure at the accomplishments of others.

Materials needed:
Chart paper and a marker.

Introduce the task:
Tell the children in your own words: *"Our Magic Circle Task today is: 'I Know Some Numbers.' Each one of you is going to get a chance to show that you know some of the numbers people use every day. First, let's review the first five."*

Present the first five numbers one at a time, saying the name of each one with the children as you write it. After each number is presented, ask the children to hold up the number of fingers it represents. (If a child holds up the wrong number of fingers, don't single him out. Hold up the correct number of your own fingers and ask the children to check for themselves.) Then ask the children to read the series of numerals with you in unison twice.

Involve the children:
Explain: *"Now I will say the name of one of the numbers and one of you will come up and point to it. Are you ready? Who would like to come up and point to the number 3?"* Select a child who volunteers. If she experiences difficulty give her hints so that she may be successful, then say: *"Good for you, (Sally)! You know the number 3!"* Next, ask the children to hold up three fingers and praise them for doing so correctly.

Continue this process until all of the children have had a chance to come up and point to a number. As each child succeeds, encourage the other children to join him in feeling pride. Occasionally ask the child who succeeded: *"How does it make you feel to get it right?"*

If the task goes quickly and the children enjoy it, do another round with the next three numbers. (If the children are ready for a greater challenge, present more numbers.) Repeat the same process of reviewing the numbers as a group, holding up the number of fingers each number represents, and allowing the children to volunteer to point to a number after you have named it. This process may be continued until you have gone through the first eight numerals (or beyond).

If the children have learned the numbers well you may introduce this more challenging variation: *"Now, who would like to point to a number I'm going to name without knowing which one it will be?"* Each time a child succeeds make a statement to him reflecting his ability to identify the correct number: *"Good job, (Ben), you pointed to the number I named! You can learn the numbers!"*

Lead a summary by asking:
1. *"What was everyone able to do?"*
2. *"How did we feel about being able to point to the right number?"*

In free-flowing discussion, allow the children to supply responses to these questions themselves.

Affirm their understanding that each child knows many numbers. The important point to emphasize is how good it feels to learn and that every day gives each one of us a chance to learn more about all sorts of things.

Conclude the Magic Circle:

Thank the children for cooperating so well in making the circle a success.

Related Activity:

Play a counting game with the children. Ask: *"How many teachers do we have in this classroom?" "How many shoes are you wearing?" "How many children are in our Magic Circle?"* Etc. Reinforce them for each correct response: *"Super job! You sure can count!"*

Unit VI

Social Development and Responsibility

Cooperating with Others

Civilization depends on cooperation yet we live in a highly competitive society. This unit offers another "hands-on" set of activities for children enabling them to focus not only on how to cooperate, but the benefits of cooperation as well.

The social nature of our lives as human beings is an inescapable reality. Unless an individual lives in complete isolation he spends much of his time living, working and playing with other people. The quality of these activities depends greatly on how well the individual is able to live, work and play in harmony with them. Developing cooperative skills entails learning to see the advantages in sharing the resources and sharing the load. The cooperative individual also learns to value the company of others. He realizes that projects and play shared by two, or more, takes on an added dimension that cannot be experienced by one person alone.

The Magic Circle is a consistent exercise in cooperation. With this unit, the focus is even more closely drawn on the dynamics of cooperative behavior and its benefits. Through repeated Magic Circle experiences, especially with those in this unit, the children come to realize that you don't have to have losers in order to have winners. When everyone wins the victory is even greater!

Magic Circle Tasks in Unit Six

"I Can Serve You"

"I Can Share a Treat with You"

"I Can Share a Tricycle with You"

"I Can Pick up Blocks with You"

"I Can Carry a Table with You"

"I Can Help You with Your Jacket"

Magic Circle Task:

"I Can Serve You"

Purpose:
In this Magic Circle the children are afforded the opportunity to discover the reciprocal nature of cooperative behavior: giving generally leads to receiving.

Materials needed:
One (possibly two) trays of food the children enjoy. For example, enough marshmallows on one tray so each child may have one and (optional) enough pieces of donut on another tray so each child may have one.

Introduce the task:
After reviewing the Magic Circle Promises and thanking the children for their attention, tell them in your own words: *"Today we're going to cooperate with each other in our Magic Circle. Do you know what cooperation is? (Take time for a brief discussion.) Our task for this Magic Circle is: 'I Can Serve You.' Each one of us will have a chance to serve another person in the circle. By serving each other we will be cooperating in a very special way. Let me show you how we will do it."*

Involve the children:
Bring out a tray of marshmallows and set it in the center of the circle. Select a child and tell the group you are going to serve him one. Then do it and replace the tray in the center of the circle. If necessary, remind the child to say thank you and ask him to hold onto his marshmallow and not to eat it yet.

Then ask the child you served how he feels about what you did. Listen to his response and then invite him to be the server. Say, *"Now you can serve me one."* After you have been served by the child, tell him it gave you a good feeling. Then ask the group, *"Who would like to go next and serve someone else in the circle?"* Call on a child and after he has served a marshmallow to another child reflect to him: *"Good, (Danny). You did a fine job of serving, (Sophia)!"* Then ask the child who was served how she feels.

Next, encourage the child who was served to serve the child who served her. Continue this procedure until everyone has served, and been served, a marshmallow, by the same person and told how it felt. Finally, eat the marshmallows together!

If time permits and interest is high, the group may experience another round, with another food the children enjoy such as pieces of donuts.

Lead a summary by asking:
1. *"What did we do today in this Magic Circle?"*
2. *"What kinds of feelings did we have?"*

Affirm the children's understanding that they cooperated with each other in that all of them served, and were served by, another person. Discuss how good it makes most people feel most of the time to be served. It makes us feel cared for. It also feels good to be the server because then we get to make someone else feel good.

Conclude the Magic Circle:
Thank the children for cooperating so well to make the Magic Circle a success.

Related Activities:
In the days following this Magic Circle, be sure to reinforce the children every time you see examples of cooperation between them. Use the word, "cooperating" when you deliver this feedback.

Suggest to the children they surprise and please the people at home by offering to serve them something they like to eat.

Magic Circle task:

"I Can Share a Treat with You"

Purpose:
In this Magic Circle the children are afforded another opportunity to experience the reciprocal nature of cooperative behavior: giving generally leads to receiving.

Materials needed:
Two trays of treats the children enjoy which can be easily shared. For example, oatmeal cookies large enough and soft enough to be easily broken in half so each child may have a half, and enough graham crackers which can easily be broken down the middle so each child may have a section.

Introduce the task:
Tell the children in your own words: *"Do you remember what we did in our last Magic Circle to make each other feel good? (The children respond.) That's right! We cooperated by serving each other! Well, today we're going to do something similar, but not quite the same. Our task is: 'I Can Share a Treat with You.' Each one of us will have someone share a treat with us and then we will share a treat with that person. Let me show you how we will do it."*

Involve the children:
Bring out a tray of treats and serve one to every other child in the circle. (These should be treats that can be easily shared.) Then tell the children: *"Sometimes it feels good to share a treat with someone else."* Demonstrate by turning to the child on your right. Ask her if she, or she, would like to share this treat with you. Assist the children as needed to break their treats in half and share them with each other so that no one is left out. Remind the children, only if necessary, to say thank you to those who shared with them. Then allow them to eat their treats. Ask the children who were shared with by another child how it felt to receive part of his treat. Discuss how good it feels to be the recipient of sharing.

Reverse the process. Ask the children who received the treats: *"Would you like to share a treat with the person who shared with you?"* Give these children a different treat for them to share and guide them through the process of sharing those treats with the children on their left. When everyone has their share of the treat, eat and enjoy them together.

Lead a summary by asking:
1. *"How does it feel to have someone share a treat with you?"*
2. *"When someone shares something with you how does it make you feel toward him, or her?"*

Affirm the children's understanding that all of them cooperated with each other. They received something from someone who shared with them, and each of them shared something with that same person. Talk about how good it makes us feel when people treat us this way. Most people feel like treating the person just as good as he treated them to show their appreciation.

Conclude the Magic Circle:
Thank the children for cooperating so well to make the Magic Circle such a success today.

Related Activity:
In the days following this Magic Circle, be sure to reinforce the children whenever you observe them sharing things with each other. Suggest that they show their families what they learned about sharing.

Magic Circle task:
"I Can Share a Tricycle with You"

Purpose:
In this Magic Circle the children are afforded the opportunity to experience the reciprocal nature of cooperative behavior in a group: giving generally leads to receiving even if one does not give to the same individual he received something from.

Materials needed:
One tricycle with a wide enough bar between the back wheels for a child to stand on and go for a ride as another pedals.

Introduce the task:
Take the children to the play area and arrange them in a semi-circle. Explain: *"Today we're going to have our Magic Circle out here. That is what will be different about this Magic Circle. We will still keep our Magic Circle Promises, though, and that is what will be the same. Do you remember how we shared treats in our last circle? Today we will share something again. Our task is: 'I Can Share a Tricycle with You.'"*

Involve the children:
Having the tricycle handy, ask for a volunteer to come and show how he makes it go. (Designate a short, close circular path.) After the child has given a brief demonstration ask: *"Is there a way (Earl) could share the tricycle with someone else?"* Hold a discussion. If no one offers the suggestion, mention that he could give someone a "standing up" ride on the back of the trike.

Next, select a second child (Melissa) to ask (Earl): *"Will you share the trike with me?"* or *"Will you give me a ride?"* After (Melissa) has been taken for a ride, ask her to tell (Earl) thanks and say how she felt about (Earl) sharing the trike with her. Then tell the second child (Melissa) to get into the driver's seat. Select another child to ask her to share the trike with him. Continue in this manner until all of the children have asked another to share the trike with them and all have shared it with another. After each ride on the trike, ask the child who was shared with to thank the other and to tell him how he felt.

Lead a summary by asking:
1. *"How does it feel to have someone share something with you?"*
2. *"When someone shares something with you how does it make you feel toward him, or her?"*

As much as possible, in free-flowing discussion, allow the children to supply responses to these questions themselves. Affirm their understanding that all of them cooperated with each other. They received a ride from someone who shared the trike with them; then they gave a ride to someone else. Talk about how good it makes us feel when people treat each other this way. Most people feel like treating the same person, and others, just as good as they were treated.

Conclude the Magic Circle:
Thank the children for cooperating so well in this Magic Circle. Suggest that they share rides with others on the tricycles they have at home

Magic Circle task:

"I Can Pick Up Blocks with You"

Purpose:
In this Magic Circle the children are afforded the opportunity to discover that cooperation between two people can cut the work in half.

Materials needed:
A container with about 40 blocks; a watch with a second hand or stop watch.

Introduce the task:
Tell the children in your own words: *"Let's start off our Magic Circle today by remembering what we did in our last three sessions. Does anyone remember?"* Discuss the treats the children served and shared with each other. Talk briefly about how these were cooperative behaviors which made them feel good. Then explain: *"Today we will cooperate with each other again in our Magic Circle, but in a different way. Our task is: 'I Can Pick Up Blocks with You.' Let me show you how we will do it."*

Involve the children:
Present the container of blocks and tell the children you would like them to watch as you conduct an experiment. Spill the blocks onto the floor in the middle of the circle. Then ask for a volunteer to pick them up. Select a child (Terry) and as he picks up the blocks time him. When he is done thank him and tell the group exactly how long it took him to do the job.

Say: *"Now, (Terry), I'd like for you to do it again, only this time ask someone to help you. While you and your helper put the blocks back into the container I will time you."* After the two children have picked up the blocks, announce to the group how long it took them and stress that it took much less time than it did when (Terry) worked alone. Ask (Terry) *"Which time did you work harder?"* and *"How would you rather pick up blocks, alone or with help?"* Finally, acknowledge (Terry) for asking for what he needed and the other child for being willing to help.

Ask the children: *"Who else would like to ask someone to help him pick up the blocks as I time you?"* Select a child who asks for help and chooses a volunteer to repeat the procedure. Continue in this vein until each child has worked with another to pick up the blocks. As each pair completes the task announce their time and ask them how they felt about having someone cooperate with them instead of having to do it alone.

Lead a summary by asking:
1. *"How did we cooperate with each other today in this Magic Circle?"*
2. *"What is so good about this kind of cooperation?"*

As much as possible, in free-flowing discussion, allow the children to supply responses to these questions themselves. Affirm their understanding that all of them cooperated with another person to do a task. Guide them to acknowledge how much easier it is for people when others cooperate with them in this way. You can get the work done in much less time and with much less effort. Not only that, when someone works with you it often turns the work into fun.

Conclude the Magic Circle:
Thank the children for cooperating so well to make the circle a big success today.

Related Activity:
In the days following this Magic Circle urge the children to help each other complete tasks by reminding them of what they learned about cooperation in this Magic Circle. Additionally, be sure to reinforce them whenever you observe them assisting each other with tasks.

Magic Circle task:

"I Can Carry a Table with You"

Purpose:
In this Magic Circle the children are afforded the opportunity to discover that cooperation between two people makes the load much lighter.

Materials needed:
Have close at hand a large and heavy enough table to present a child with a struggle if he tried to move it alone.

Introduce the task:
Tell the children in your own words: *"Let's start off our Magic Circle today by remembering what we did in our last session. Does anyone remember?"* Discuss the way in which the children cooperated with each other by picking up blocks together. Then explain: *"Today we will cooperate with each other again in our Magic Circle, but in a different way. Our task is: 'I Can Carry a Table with You.' Let's all get up and move over here by this table. And I will show you how we will do it."*

Ask the children: *"Have you ever noticed how hard it is to move a table by yourself?"* Demonstrate with the table while they watch. Then say: *"Many times we need to do something, such as move a table like this, but we are not able to do it very well on our own. That is when we need to ask someone to help us."*

Involve the children:
Take hold of one end of the table and ask: *"Who would like to help me carry this table?"* Select a volunteer and have him take hold of the other end. Before carrying the table inform the child where you want to take it. For example: *"Let's carry the table over to the carpet, okay?"* Then direct him to lift his end as you lift yours and carefully walk sideways together carrying the table to its destination. Thank the child for his willingness to cooperate and tell him how good it made you feel when he volunteered to help you out.

Then ask the child if he would like to ask for someone to help him move the table back to its original spot again. Direct him to select a volunteer and to move the table back to its original location. Guide these two children through the process you just undertook with the first child, being sure to have the child thank his volunteer for the help he gave. Continue this procedure, moving the table back and forth, until the last child asks for help with the table. At that point volunteer to help him. Then everyone will have had a turn to help, and to ask for help, with moving the table.

Lead a summary by asking:
1. *"How did we cooperate with each other today in this Magic Circle?"*
2. *"What is so good about this kind of cooperation?"*

As much as possible, in free-flowing discussion, allow the children to supply responses to these questions themselves. Affirm their understanding that all of them cooperated with another person to do a task. Guide them to acknowledge how much easier it is for people when others cooperate with them in this way. You can get the work done so much more easily and quickly. Not only that, when someone helps you a hard job often becomes a fun experience.

Conclude the Magic Circle:
Thank the children for cooperating so well in this Magic Circle.

Related Activity:
Suggest to the children that they watch for chances at home when they could help family members with tasks. Suggest that people can always use help when they are cleaning up a room, making a bed, or sweeping a floor. Discuss how helping them will probably make the person feel very good.

Magic Circle task:

"I Can Help You with Your Jacket"

Purpose:
In this Magic Circle the children are afforded the opportunity to discover that cooperation between two people can make an awkward struggle go smoothly with very little effort.

Materials needed:
One child's jacket that fits all of the children.

Introduce the task:
Tell the children in your own words: *"Let's start off our Magic Circle today by remembering what we did in our last two sessions. Does anyone remember?"* Discuss how the children discovered that if they help each other with tasks like picking up blocks and carrying a table, it makes the work a lot easier, quicker and more pleasant. Then explain: *"Today we will cooperate with each other again in our Magic Circle. Our task is: 'I Can Help You with Your Jacket.' Here's (Howie's) jacket. He has agreed to let us use it. Let me show you how."*

Hold up the jacket and ask the children, *"Have you ever noticed how hard it is sometimes to put on a jacket and to take it off when you don't have any help? It can be tough! But there's a way one person can help another and we're going to get a chance to practice. Let's see how one person can help another put a jacket on and take it off again."*

Involve the children:
Ask: *"Who would like to help me with a demonstration?"* Select a child and ask him to put the jacket on without help from anyone while the group watches. His struggle will probably be amusing. Then suggest to the child that he could ask for help. As soon as he asks, be the volunteer. Tell the other children to watch closely to see how you help him because they will get a chance soon and will need to know how to do it. As you demonstrate, tell them: *"I help him by holding the jacket up and moving it so his first arm goes in easily. Then I help him with the second arm by guiding it into the sleeve."*

After the child has the jacket fully on have him ask you to help him take it off. Tell the children: *"This is very easy. All you have to do to help someone get a jacket off is to hold firmly onto the end of one of his sleeves and he will do the rest."* Demonstrate. (If necessary, remind the child to say thanks.) Then ask the child, *"Was it easier when I helped you?"*

Ask the children: *"Who would like to go next?"* Hand the jacket to the child you select and then guide him and the helper he selects through the same process you just went through with the first child. Continue in this manner until each child has had a turn to be the helper and the "helpee."

Lead a summary by asking:
1. *"How did we cooperate with each other today in this Magic Circle?"*
2. *"What is so good about this kind of cooperation?"*

As much as possible, in free-flowing discussion, allow the children to supply responses to these questions themselves. Affirm their understanding that all of them cooperated with another person by helping him with the everyday struggle of putting on, and taking off, a jacket. Guide them to acknowledge how much easier it is for people when we ask for help and give help. Often the help we give is extremely simple for us to do, yet makes a big difference to the person we have helped.

Conclude the Magic Circle:

Thank the children for cooperating so well to make the circle a big success today.

Related Activity:

Create a "buddy system" for the purpose of encouraging the children to help each other with a variety of classroom challenges. The first "assignment" for the "buddies" might be for them to help each other take off their jackets when they arrive at school each day and put them on again when it's time to go home.

Unit VII

Self Awareness

Experiencing and Expressing Our Feelings

Feelings are the prime movers of behavior. It is through our feelings that we interpret the quality of our inner and outer worlds. As such, this unit which acknowledges human emotion is very important.

We believe awareness and acceptance of feelings are vital because they are necessary in the development of self understanding and self control. When an individual can "talk to himself" and name his feelings he does not push them below the surface only to have them come up later in undesirable ways. The individual can decide what to do with the energy his feelings generate. He can control his impulses while not denying his emotions to himself.

A key outcome of the Magic Circle process is children's increased awareness and acceptance of feelings, their own and those of others. This unit doubles that effort by focusing directly on feelings through its content. All six topics elicit responses from children which relate to pleasant feelings. Unpleasant feelings are noted by the leader in the introduction of the topic.

Magic Circle Topics in Unit Seven

"I Can Show You Something in the Room that I Feel Good About"

"Something in the Box that Gives Me Good Feelings"

"I Can Show You Something from Home that I Feel Good About"

"Something I Do at School that Makes Me Feel Good"

"Something I Do At Home that Makes Me Feel Good"

"A Favorite Place Where I Feel Good"

Magic Circle Topic:

"I Can Show You Something in the Room that I Feel Good About"

Purpose:

Each child is given a chance in this Magic Circle to identify an object and to describe the positive feelings he has about it. This process gives the children the opportunity to learn that each individual has his own preferences and feelings. This understanding leads to self acceptance and acceptance of others.

Introduce the topic:

After reviewing the Magic Circle Promises tell the children in your own words: *"Our topic for this Magic Circle is: 'I Can Show You Something in the Room that I Feel Good About.' At times everybody has good feelings and at other times we all have feelings that aren't so good. Today we are going to talk about our good feelings. We are going to show each other things in our classroom we feel good about. Won't that be fun?*

"Let me show you how to do it. I will go first. I'm looking around the room and thinking about something that I like. It's something that gives me a good feeling. (Demonstrate that you are viewing the objects in the room and then thinking about one thing you like by looking at the item for several seconds.) *I've thought of the thing that gives me a good feeling. Now I'm going to go get it and bring it to the circle and show it to you."* Upon your return to the circle with your item, show it to the children and tell them in a few words why the item gives you a good feeling.

Involve the children:

Ask for volunteers: *"Who else is thinking of something you like in our room? Who would like to go get it, bring it over, show it to us, and tell us how you feel about it?"*

As the children volunteer, be sure they have an item in mind before they leave the circle. If the process moves slowly and the waiting children become restless you could allow two children to go for their items at a time. When the child whose turn it is returns to the circle, engage her in friendly conversation in front of the group. *"Well, well, (Gina) brought a book to show us. What book is it (Gina)? Tell us about it. How do you feel about this book and its story? What is your favorite part?"* When a child's turn is completed excuse her to return the object to it's original location.

Conduct a review (optional) by saying:

"Let's see how well we can remember. Some (or all) of us brought something from the room to the circle. We brought things that give us good feelings. Who remembers what (Gina) brought?" Call on individual children to tell each other what they brought to the circle.

As each one reviews to another, reinforce the child: *"What a good memory you have! You didn't forget that (Gina) brought a book [name title] for us to see. Now, does anybody remember why (Gina) said she liked it?"* Reinforce again those who remember what other children said and be sure each child who spoke during the session is reviewed to.

Lead a summary by asking:

1. *"How did we feel about the things we brought to the circle to show each other?"*
2. *"Can you think of any other words that say we felt good?"*
3. *"Did we all feel good about the very same thing? Is it okay for each of us to feel good about something different?"*

As much as possible, in free-flowing discussion, allow the children to supply responses to these questions themselves. Affirm their understanding that the things brought to the circle produced pleasant feelings in each individual who selected them. Help the children generate other vocabulary for good feelings, such as "happy," "pleasant," "super," or "wonderful," etc. Finally, assist them to understand that each person is an individual and has his own feelings. That's what makes each of us unique and special.

Conclude the Magic Circle:

Thank the children for sharing and listening and for making the circle a success.

Related Activity:

Organize a short "hands-on" sharing time. Divide the class into three or four subgroups to go with three or four "child leaders." The leaders will share the item they brought to the group. For example, three children could go with Gina as Gina reads the story in the book she brought to the group to them. Three other children could go to the clay table with a child who brought clay to the Magic Circle. Etc.

Hold an informal discussion with the children about caring for the items they like in the classroom.

Magic Circle Topic:

"Something in the Box that Gives Me Good Feelings"

Purpose:

Each child is given a chance to imagine an object within a box and describe his positive feelings about it in this Magic Circle. This process affords the children the opportunity to understand that each person has his own preferences and feelings. This realization leads to self acceptance and acceptance of others.

Materials Needed:

One empty box with lid in place.

Introduce the topic:

Tell the children in your own words: *"Our topic for this Magic Circle is: 'Something in the Box that Gives Me Good Feelings.' Sometimes we have pleasant feelings and sometimes we have unpleasant feelings. Today we're going to talk again about pleasant feelings. We're going to get to use our imaginations to help us think about things that give us good feelings. We'll get a chance to tell each other what those things are and the kinds of pleasant feelings they give us."*

Hold up empty box with lid in place and tell the group: *"You can see I've a box here and it is empty."* Open the box and show that it is empty inside. Then replace the lid and say: *"Let's have some fun with this box and imagine that it isn't empty. Each of us can make a picture in our mind of something that could be in the box that would make us feel very good. It could be a toy of some kind, or an animal, or maybe something to eat. And your feelings could be 'super,' or 'happy,' or 'excited,' or some other good feeling.*

"Can you think of something like that? Something you would like to find in this box? Let's close our eyes and use our imaginations. Make a picture in your mind of the thing you wish was in the box. Just think for a moment or two. When you are ready to tell us about what would give you good feelings if it was in the box, open your eyes and look at me. Then I'll know you are ready to talk and listen."

Involve the children:

Demonstrate that you are imagining something you would like to find in the box by closing your eyes and concentrating for several seconds. If the children are not ready to speak, take your turn first: *"I've thought of something I'd really like to find in the box that would give me a good feeling. Let me tell you about it..."* Then invite the children to take turns telling what they would like to find in the box. *"Who would like to tell us about something you would like to find in the box that would give you good feelings? Raise your hand if you are ready."*

As necessary, ask open-ended questions to individual children as they share, but do so sparingly: *"Tell us what you would like to do if you found a ball in the box, (Karen)? Tell us about the ball; what would it be like? How would you feel if it was really in there? What is it like for you when you play with that kind of ball?"*

Demonstrate an accepting attitude to what the children say. It is likely they will mention things that would never fit inside the box and that is okay. They may also imitate each others' responses.

Conduct a review (optional) by saying:

"Let's see how well we listened to each other. Some (or all) of us told about something we would like to find in the box that would give us good feelings. Who remembers what (Karen) told us about?"

One by one call on the children to individually tell each other what they heard each other say, and as they do, reinforce them: *"(Karen), didn't (Harold) listen well to you? Now, does anybody remember what it's like for (Karen) when she plays with a ball like that?"* Reinforce again those who remember specific feelings and be sure each child who spoke during the session is reviewed to.

Lead a summary by asking:

1. *"How did we feel about the things we imagined might be in the box?"*
2. *"What kinds of good feelings did we say we would have if the things we like were in the box? Can you think of any other words that say 'good'?"*
3. *"Did we all want the very same thing to be in the box? Is it okay for each of us to feel good about different things?"*

As much as possible, in free-flowing discussion, allow the children to supply responses to these questions themselves. Guide them to focus on the fact that everyone experienced positive feelings about the object imagined and described. Assist them to generate other vocabulary, such as "happy," "satisfied," "thrilled," or "pleased." Finally, help them to understand that each person is an individual and has his own preferences and feelings. Understanding this aspect of human nature makes us tolerant and respectful of each other.

Prepare for the Next Magic Circle: Tell the children that the Magic Circle topic for our next session will be: *"I Can Show You Something from Home that I Feel Good About."* In preparation ask them to bring something from home, some favorite item they would like to show the other children. It may be a good idea to send a note home explaining what will occur in the next Magic Circle asking the parents to assist their children to select something and to make sure it is brought to school on the right day. (You may decide to begin these preparations several days in advance of that session.)

Conclude the Magic Circle:

Thank the children for sharing and listening and for making the circle a success.

Related Activity:

As a group, make up a song/chant or poem related to this topic. Here's a suggestion for a start:

> Something in the box!
> Something in the box!
> That gives us good feelings!
> Karen wants a big blue ball!
> Mike wants fried chicken!
> Susan likes a tiny doll!
> Tom, a guitar for pickin'!
> (Etc.)

Magic Circle Topic:

"I Can Show You Something from Home that I Feel Good About"

Purpose:

In this Magic Circle each child is given the opportunity to show the other children an item brought from home and to tell them how he feels about it. This process gives the children a chance to learn that each individual has his own preferences and feelings. This understanding leads to self acceptance and acceptance of others.

Materials Needed:

Items from home the children have brought.

Introduce the topic:

Tell the children in your own words: *"Our Magic Circle topic for this session is: 'I Can Show You Something from Home that I Feel Good About.' It's true that everyone has unpleasant feelings at times, but today we are going to talk about our good feelings again. Do you remember I asked each of you to bring something from home you feel good about? We are going to show each other the things we brought. Won't that be fun?*

"Let me show you how we will do it. I will go first. Here is what I brought from home. It's something that gives me a good feeling." Show the children the item you brought from home and tell them in a few words why the item gives you a good feeling. Be sure to use a variety of words to describe how you feel about the object.

Involve the children:

Ask for volunteers: *"Who else would like to show us what you brought from home that gives you good feelings?"* As necessary, ask open-ended questions to individual children as they share, but do so sparingly: *"Why does this item make you feel so good?"* or *"Why is this special to you?"*

Lead a summary by asking:

1. *"How did we feel about the things we brought from home to show each other?"*
2. *"Can you think of any other words that say we felt good?"*
3. *"Did we all feel good about the very same things? Is it okay for us to feel good about different things?"*

In free-flowing discussion, allow the children to supply responses to these questions themselves. Affirm their understanding that the things brought from home produced pleasant feelings in each individual who selected them. Help them generate other vocabulary for good feelings, such as "happy," "pleasant," "super," or "wonderful." Finally, assist them to understand that each person is an individual and has his own preferences and feelings. That's what makes each of us unique and special.

Conclude the Magic Circle:

Thank the children for sharing and listening and for making the circle a success.

Related Activity:

Organize a short "hands-on" sharing time. Divide the group into three or four subgroups each having a "child leader." The "child leaders" are individual children who brought items from home that could be shared with one or more other children. For example, Gary may share the game he brought from home with two other children. Ted may read the story in a book he brought with three others. Etc.

Magic Circle Topic:

"Something I Do at School that Makes Me Feel Good"

Purpose:

The children are each given a chance to identify and describe an activity they enjoy at school in this Magic Circle. This gives them the opportunity to learn that each individual has his own preferences and feelings. This understanding leads to self acceptance and acceptance of others.

Introduce the topic:

In your own words say: *"Today our Magic Circle topic is: 'Something I Do at School that Makes Me Feel Good.' Everybody likes to feel good and everybody has good feelings at times. Sometimes we call our good feelings 'nice,' 'pleasant,' 'wonderful,' or 'super.' Everybody also feels unpleasant feelings at times. But today we are going to talk about good feelings. We are going to have a chance to tell each other about something we like to do at school that feels good when we do it. Can you think of something like that? Something you like to do because you feel nice, or wonderful or happy?*

"Let's close our eyes and use our memories. Let's remember things we like to do at school. Can you remember doing something here that gave you good feelings? Just think for a moment or two. When you are ready to tell us about something you do at school that gives you good feelings, open your eyes and look at me. Then I'll know you are ready to talk and listen."

Involve the children:

If the children are not ready to speak, take your turn first. You could say something like this: *"I've thought of something I like to do here at school, something that gives me a good feeling. Let me tell you about it..."* Then invite the children to take turns to speak: *"Who would like to tell us about something you like to do here that gives you good feelings? Raise your hand if you are ready."*

As necessary, ask open-ended questions to individual children as they share: *"Tell us how you feel when you are painting at the easel. How do you play tag with your friends? What is it like for you when you play with our wooden train?"* Etc.

Lead a summary by asking:

1. *"How do we feel about the things we do that we told each other about?"*

2. *"What kinds of good feelings do we have when we do these things at school? Can you think of any other words that say how we feel?"*

3. *"Did we all feel good about doing the very same things? Is it okay for us to feel good about doing different things?"*

As children respond, affirm their understanding that everyone experienced positive feelings about the activities they described. Assist them to generate other vocabulary, such as "excited," "thrilled," "pleased," or "happy." Finally, help them to acknowledge that each person is an individual and has his own preferred activities and feelings. If we were all the same we wouldn't be so interesting to each other.

Conclude the Magic Circle:

Thank the children for sharing and listening and for making the circle a success.

Related Activity:

Ask the children to make a picture of themselves doing the things they like to do at school. Display their pictures with captions that are direct quotations from what they said during the circle. As a group, look at the display. Read each caption aloud to the group. Then read it together.

Magic Circle Topic:

"Something I Do at Home that Makes Me Feel Good"

Purpose:

This Magic Circle affords each child a chance to describe an enjoyable activity he experiences at home. The fact that each individual identifies an activity uniquely meaningful to him is brought to the children's attention. This understanding leads to self acceptance and acceptance of others.

Introduce the topic:

Tell the children in your own words: *"Our topic for this Magic Circle is: ''Something I Do At Home that Makes Me Feel Good.' Everybody has pleasant feelings at times and unpleasant feelings at other times. Today we are going to talk about pleasant feelings again. We will share our good feelings which we sometimes call 'nice,' 'pleasant,' 'wonderful,' or 'super,' and other words like these. We are going to have a chance to tell each other about something we like to do at home that feels good when we do it. Think of something like that?*

"Let's close our eyes and use our memories. Remember things we like to do at home that feel good. Can you remember doing something like that? Think for a moment or two. When you are ready to tell us about something you do at home that gives you good feelings, open your eyes and look at me. Then I'll know you are ready to talk and listen."

Involve the children:

Demonstrate that you are imagining something you like to do at home by closing your eyes and concentrating for several seconds. If the children are not ready to speak, take your turn first: *"I've thought of something I like to do at home that gives me a good feeling. Let me tell you about it..."* Then invite the children to share: *"Who would like to tell us about something you like to do at home because it gives you good feelings? Raise your hand if you are ready."*

As necessary, ask open-ended questions, but do so sparingly. You could say something like this: *"How do you feel when you are playing a computer game?"* or *"How do you play in the sand pile with your brother or sister?"*

Lead a summary by asking:

1. *"How did we feel about the things we do at home that we told each other about?"*

2. *"What kinds of good feelings do we have when we do these fun things at home? Can you think of other words that say how we feel?"*

Affirm the children's understanding that everyone experienced positive feelings about the activities they described. Assist them to generate other vocabulary, such as "excited," "thrilled," "pleased," or "pumped." Finally, help them to understand that each person is an individual and has his own preferred activities and feelings. If we were all the same we wouldn't be so interesting to each other.

Conclude the Magic Circle:

Thank the children for sharing and listening and for making the circle a success.

Related Activity:

Ask the children to draw a picture of themselves doing the enjoyable things at home. Have them draw their pictures on one side of a paper you have folded in half. As the children create their drawings, ask each one to tell you about his picture. On the blank side of the paper write what the child says verbatim. Read it with the child until he can read it by himself. At the end of the day, send the pictures home. Ask the children to talk about their drawings and read their stories to their parents and siblings.

Magic Circle Topic:

"A Favorite Place Where I Feel Good"

Purpose:

In this Magic Circle each child is given a chance to identify a place and to describe how he feels when he is there. This process gives the children the opportunity to learn that each individual has his own preferences and feelings. This understanding leads to self acceptance and acceptance of others.

Introduce the topic:

In your own words tell the children: *"Today our Magic Circle topic is: 'A Favorite Place Where I Feel Good.' I am feeling good because I am here in our classroom with you. I like each one of you very much and I like this place. This is a special place for me; it gives me warm and happy feelings. There are some places I don't like to be very much, but this is a place I really do like. There are other places I like too, places that make me feel comfortable, or excited, or content.*

"In our circle today we are going to have a chance to tell each other about places we like to be; places where we feel good. Can you think of a place like that? Maybe there are some people in the place who are nice to you and love you. Maybe they take good care of you and so you just feel wonderful being there. Perhaps the place you think of is an exciting or beautiful place and you like the way you feel when you are there. Maybe you go exploring. Maybe it has lots of goodies, like the library which is full of good books, or someone else's back yard which has some new toys. Maybe you are like me, and one of your favorite places is here in our classroom.

"Let's close our eyes and think. Let's ask ourselves about our favorite places to be, places that give us good feelings. Then choose one place in your mind to tell us about. We'd like to know where the place is. We'd also like to know why it is one of your favorite places and how you feel when you are there. Just think for a moment or two. When you are ready to talk, open your eyes and look at me. Then I'll know you are ready to talk and listen."

Involve the children:

Demonstrate that you are thinking about a favorite place of your own by closing your eyes and concentrating for several seconds. If the children are not ready to speak, take your turn first. You could say something like this: *"I've thought of a favorite place of my own that gives me good feelings. Let me tell you about it..."* Then invite the children to take turns to speak: *"Who would like to tell us about a place that gives you good feelings? Raise your hand if you are ready."*

As necessary, ask open-ended questions to individual children as they share, but do so sparingly: *"Tell us how you feel when you are there?"* or *"What is it like for you to be there?"*

Since this topic is less concrete than some others in this unit, do not be surprised if the children copy each other. Simply demonstrate an accepting attitude.

Conduct a review (optional) by saying:

"Let's see how well we can remember. Some (or all) of us told about a favorite place where we like to be. Raise your hand if you can remember what (Leonard) told us about?" Call on individual children to tell each other what they told about.

As each one reviews to another, reinforce the child: *"You listened very well, (Joe)! Does anybody remember what kinds of good feelings (Leonard) says he has when he is at Barbara's house?"* Reinforce again those who remember specific positive feelings reported. Be sure each child who spoke during the session receives a review.

Lead a summary by asking:

1. *"How did we feel about the places we told each other about?"*

2. *"What kinds of good feelings do we have when we are in our favorite places? Can you think of any other words that say how we feel about these places?"*

3. *"Did we all feel good about the very same place? Is it okay if we have different favorite places?"*

As much as possible, in free-flowing discussion, allow the children to supply responses to these questions themselves. Affirm their understanding that everyone experienced positive feelings about being in the places they described. Assist them to generate other vocabulary, such as "content," "satisfied," "liked," "loved," "cared for," etc. Finally, focus on how natural and normal it is for different people to have different (and sometimes the same) favorite places. This is because we are uniquely affected by different physical and human environments.

Conclude the Magic Circle:

Thank the children for sharing and listening and for making the circle a success.

Related Activity:

Ask the children to draw pictures of themselves in their favorite places. Display their pictures under the heading, "Our Favorite Places." View the display as a group. As you focus on each child's picture ask him to tell the group about it. Write what he says on a strip of paper and place it under his picture. Then read the caption aloud and invite the children to read it with you aloud.

Unit VIII

Self Management

Taking Pride in Our Accomplishments

This unit is offered to provide the children with an initial experience in developing positive "self talk" and benefiting from the power it brings.

Small children behave and feel all of the time, but it is rare for a child to identify or assess his actions and feelings to himself. Moreover, the relationship between one's actions and the feelings about oneself those actions engender, is particularly remote from awareness not only for small children but for many adults as well. Generally, one's behavior is "shaped" by significant others who react to it; self-confidence or self-disdain result from whether or not those reactions are positive most of the time or negative most of the time. Thus, the individual often misses the connection between his actions and his feelings about himself, and without realizing it places this responsibility in the hands of others.

It is a vital mental activity, therefore, to be able to "talk to oneself" to identify constructive, self-enhancing actions and those which are self-destructive, to take deserved pride in one's accomplishments, to develop compassion for one's mistakes and to decide to learn from them. Through this process an individual is enabled to become instrumental in building his own self awareness and self-management skills.

The Magic Circles in this unit offer the children repeated opportunities to tell each other about times they handled situations which challenged them. Because feedback from significant others is enormously influential, the group's attention, acceptance and appreciation shown to each child for sharing his accomplishment, makes a strong impact. Through this repetitive process each child may recognize how he has already behaved in effective ways which implies his ability to do it again. Each child also receives numerous ideas for ways to behave effectively in the future by listening to his peers and by listening to you.

Magic Circle Topics in Unit Eight

"A Game I Learned to Play"

"A Time I Took Care of Myself"

"I Thought I Could Do It and I Did"

"A Time I Kept Trying And Then I Could Do It"

"A Time I Did It All By Myself"

"A Time My Mistake Helped Me Learn"

Magic Circle Topic:

"A Game I Learned to Play"

Purpose:

This Magic Circle affords each child the opportunity to develop self awareness and to build her own self-esteem by mentally identifying one of her accomplishments (learning to play a game) and then telling others about it. In the process she is enabled to understand the benefits of behaving effectively. She also gains many ideas along these lines from her peers.

Introduce the topic:

After reviewing the Magic Circle Promises and thanking the children for their attention, tell them in your own words: *"Today we are going to have a chance to tell each other about something we were able to do. We call things we are able to do 'accomplishments.' Let's all say that word together."*

"Our topic is: 'A Game I Learned to Play.' There are lots of games and many of them are so much fun. Games also teach us things. They teach us how to play with others and how to think better. They also teach us about ourselves; they give us a chance to show what we can do. Learning how to play a game is an accomplishment."

"Think for a bit about a game you can play. You can play it because you learned how in some way. This could be any kind of game like tag, or Simon Says, or Chinese Checkers. Think about the game; think of it's name; how you learned to play it; and how you feel when you play it. If you would like to tell us about it, we would like to hear. Let's close our eyes and think. When you open them I'll know you are ready to talk and listen."

Involve the children:

Demonstrate that you are thinking about the topic by closing your eyes and concentrating for several seconds. Invite the children to raise their hands when they are ready to share. If no one is ready, take your own turn. You might tell about a game you learned to play when you were their age. For example: *"When I was (four) years old I learned to play a game at school called 'Drop the Handkerchief.' It was fun. All the children formed a big circle as one child skipped around behind us. That child was called, 'it' and then he dropped a handkerchief behind one person in the circle. That person ran after him and tried to catch him. If he caught him he went back to his spot in the circle and the same child was still 'it.' If he didn't catch him he became 'it.' I used to enjoy being chosen by the person who was 'it' because it was more fun for me to run than to stand and watch."*

"Now, who would like to tell us about a game you learned to play?" As the children speak, model effective listening skills. As necessary, help each one tell the group about the game he learned to play with the use of open-ended questions: *"Tell us how you learned to play 'Hide and Go Seek,' (Carrie)."* *"What part of the game do you like best?"* As each child completes his turn, acknowledge his contribution: *"Thanks (Garrett). It was good of you to tell us how you learned to play 'Spoons.'"* (Do not be surprised if the children copy each other. Simply demonstrate an accepting attitude.)

Conduct a review (Optional) by saying:

"Let's see how well we listened to each other. Who can remember what (Carrie's) game was? Raise your hand." Guide the children to tell each other what they heard each other say in this manner, asking also about the feelings the children remember hearing each other report in relation to the game they learned to play.

Reinforce the children for their listening abilities: *"Good for you! You remembered that (Carrie) told us she felt excited when she plays*

'Hide and Go Seek' with her brothers and sisters!" Be sure everyone who shared during the circle is reviewed to, including yourself.

Lead a summary by asking:

1. *"What did we do in our Magic Circle today?"*
2. *"Is it good for us to know when we have accomplished something like learning how to play a game?"*
3. *"Is it an accomplishment to be able to share in the Magic Circle?"*

As much as possible, in free-flowing discussion, allow the children to supply responses to these questions themselves. Affirm their understanding that they told about the accomplishment of learning to play a game. Being able to tell about it is also an accomplishment. It's good for us to know when we have accomplished something and for us to feel good about ourselves when we do it. We can say to ourselves: *"Self, you did a good job. You accomplished something!"*

Conclude the Magic Circle:

Thank the children for sharing and listening so well to make the circle a success.

Related Activity:

Ask the children to draw pictures of themselves playing the games they told about in the Magic Circle. Post their pictures on a bulletin board or large folding cardboard display with captions telling about the artist and his game. For example,

Carrie learned to play Hide and Seek!

Garrett learned to play Spoons!

Etc.

The next day gather the children to view the display with you. Look at each picture and point out something delightful about it. Read each caption to the children and then ask them to read it with you in unison.

Magic Circle Topic:

"A Time I Took Care of Myself"

Purpose:

This Magic Circle affords each child the opportunity to build his own self-esteem and self-confidence by mentally identifying one of his accomplishments (meeting one of his own physical needs) and then telling others about it. In the process he is enabled to understand the benefits of behaving effectively. He also gains many ideas along these lines from his peers.

Introduce the Topic:

Tell the children in your own words: *"Today we are going to have a chance to tell each other about another accomplishment. Do you remember what an accomplishment is? (The children respond.) Right! It's something you work at that turns out well."*

"Our topic is 'A Time I Took Care of Myself.' You are taking care of yourself anytime you do something for yourself that someone else, like your mother, used to have to do for you when you were younger."

"Let's think for a bit about how we can take care of ourselves. Children can take care of themselves at home and at school and they can do it in lots of ways. Maybe you were hungry and your mother was busy so you took care of yourself by getting something to eat. Or perhaps you were getting dressed and instead of having someone else zip your zipper, you did it for yourself. We would like to hear how you have taken care of yourself and how you felt when you did it. So if you want to share you may. Let's close our eyes and think. When you open them I'll know you are ready to talk and listen."

Involve the children:

Demonstrate that you are thinking about the topic by closing your eyes and concentrating for several seconds. Then invite the children to raise their hands when they are ready to speak. If no one is ready, take your own turn. You might tell about a way in which you cared for yourself when you were their age. For example: *"When I was (five) years old I used to make my own bed. It was hard, but my brother and I made a deal. I helped him with his bed and then he helped me with mine. (It's much easier when two people do it together.) I always felt good about being able to do that for myself instead of having my mother do it for me. I felt so grown up. Besides, when my bed was made I could put things on it without having them get lost in the covers. And it looked good.*

"Now, who would like to tell us, or maybe even show us, a way you took care of yourself?" As the children speak, model effective listening skills. As necessary, help each one tell the group about how she can care for herself with the use of open-ended questions: *"What did you do for yourself, (Maria)?" "Tell us about how you brushed your own hair." "How did it feel when you did it for yourself without help from someone else?"* As each child completes his turn, acknowledge his contribution: *"That was interesting, (Ted). You helped us understand how to tie our own shoes."*

Lead a summary by asking:

1. *"What did we do in our Magic Circle today?"*

2. *"Is it good for us to know when we have accomplished something like taking care of ourselves in some way?"*

3. *"Is it an accomplishment to be able to share in the Magic Circle?"*

As much as possible, in free-flowing discussion, allow the children to supply responses to these questions themselves. Affirm their understanding that they told about the accomplishment of taking care of themselves. Being able to tell about it is also an accomplishment. It's good for us to know when we have accomplished something and for us to feel good about ourselves when we do it. We can say to ourselves: *"Good for you, self. That was an accomplishment!"*

Conclude the Magic Circle:

Thank the children for sharing and listening so well to make the circle a success.

Related Activity:

Create a chant with the children reflecting the ways in which they took care of themselves. It could go something like this:

> We can take care of ourselves!
>
> We can take care of ourselves!
>
> Maria brushes her hair and that's an accomplishment!
>
> Ted ties his own shoes and that's an accomplishment!.

Magic Circle Topic:

"I Thought I Could Do It and I Did"

Purpose:

In this Magic Circle the children will have the opportunity to mentally identify, and talk about, instances when they were aided in meeting a challenge by their own self-confidence and persistence.

Precede this Magic Circle by reading the classic storybook, *"The Little Engine That Could,"* to the children. This delightful classic is about a little train engine who managed to make a very steep grade because he thought he could and he didn't give up. (Written by Wattie Piper and illustrated by George and Doris Hauman, New York: Platt & Munk, a division of Grossett & Dunlap).

Introduce the topic:

Tell the children in your own words: *"Today our Magic Circle topic is: 'I Thought I Could Do It and I Did.' It's a very special topic because it gives us a chance to think of times when we knew we could do something and, sure enough, we did do it. Can you think of a time like that?*

"Give it some thought. Maybe you were trying to learn to do something new like slide down a great big scary slide, and you knew you could do it so you tried even though you were scared, and you found out that you could! Or perhaps you were trying to accomplish something at school like drawing an animal and you weren't sure how to do it, but you thought you probably could so you tried it, and it turned out fine. If you think of a time when you thought you could do something and, sure enough you could, and you would like to tell us about it, we would like to listen to you. Let's close our eyes and think for a bit; when you're looking at me, I'll know you're ready to share and listen to others."

Involve the children:

Demonstrate that you are thinking about the topic by closing your eyes and concentrating for several seconds. Since this topic is somewhat complex the children may not be sure how to respond. If this occurs take your turn first. You might say something like this: *"I remember the time when I was (four) years old and I wanted to be able to do somersaults. I saw my friend doing somersaults and so I thought to myself, 'I'll bet I could do that too' and so I tried. My first somersaults weren't too good. It sure felt funny when I bunched up my body and rolled over again and again. But I practiced and I got better; pretty soon I was doing some good somersaults. I thought I could do it and I did! I felt proud of myself!*

"Now who else can think of a time when you thought you could do something and so you tried, and maybe it was hard, but you did it anyway?" As the children share, assist them only as needed by asking open-ended questions: *"What happened when you first tried to skate, (Fred)?" "What did you say to yourself?" "How does it work out now when you ride the pony, (Gina)?"* When each child completes his remarks, thank him and reflect to him what he was able to do because he thought he could: *"Thanks, (Fred). It was interesting to hear how you learned to skate. You thought you could do it and, sure enough after trying hard, you did!"*

Lead a summary by asking:

1. "What did we talk about in our Magic Circle today?"

2. "Do you think it helped us to think we could do the things we told about before we tried them?"

As much as possible, in free-flowing discussion, allow the children to supply responses to these questions themselves. Affirm their understanding that those who shared in the circle told us how they did something they thought they could do. Guide them to recognize that thinking you can do something certainly does help you do it, even if it is difficult and your first tries don't work too well. Whenever you want to try something you can say to yourself: *"Self, you can do it; don't give up!"* Then you can say to yourself: *"Self, keep doing it; you will get better!"*

Conclude the Magic Circle:

Thank the children for sharing and listening; it made the circle a big success.

Related Activity:

Follow this Magic Circle by creating a chant with the children based on *"The Little Engine That Could,"* and inserting lines regarding the children's accomplishments. For example:

Fred said, "I think I can, I think I can, I think I can!"

Fred learned to roller skate.

Then he said, "I thought I could, I thought I could, I thought I could!"

Gina said, "I think I can, I think I can, I think I can!"

Gina learned to ride a pony.

Then she said, "I thought I could, I thought I could, I thought I could!"

Magic Circle Topic:

"A Time I Kept Trying and Then I Could Do It"

Purpose:

This Magic Circle affords each child the opportunity to build his own self-confidence by mentally identifying a time he learned to do something because he had the tenacity and discipline to keep trying. In the process he is enabled to understand the benefits of attempting certain tasks over and over again. He also gains many ideas along these lines from his peers.

Introduce the topic:

Tell the children in your own words: *"Our topic for this Magic Circle is: 'A Time I Kept Trying and Then I Could Do It.' Today we will have a chance to talk about something we were not able to do at first, but we kept trying until we could finally do it. Can you think of anything like that? Maybe it was something you learned to do with your body. Perhaps you saw some children skipping and you wanted to skip too but you found out that's it's pretty hard. So maybe you kept watching to see how they did it, and you kept trying, and then finally you were doing it!*

"Let's close our eyes for a minute. Think of something you couldn't do at first, but by trying it over and over again you finally learned to do it. When you remember something like that, and if you would like to tell us about it, we would like to hear your story. When you are ready open your eyes and look at me. Then I'll know you are ready to talk and listen."

Involve the children:

Demonstrate that you are thinking about the topic by closing your eyes and concentrating for several seconds. If the children are not ready to speak, take your turn first. You could say something like this: *"I don't remember being a baby, but my mother told me all about how I learned to walk. She said I would hold onto something while I stood up and then I would try to walk by taking one step and then trying to take another before I fell down. She said I did it over and over again; then later I could walk several steps before I fell down. Finally, I walked just fine and before she knew it I was running. I'll bet each of you learned to walk when you were babies just about the same way."*

Invite the children to take turns to speak: *"Who would like to tell us about something you kept trying to do and then you could do it? Raise your hand if you are ready."* As necessary, ask open-ended questions to individual children as they share, but do so sparingly: *"What was it like for you when you kept trying and trying so hard?" "Tell us how you felt when you were finally able to do it?"* After a child has completed his turn, acknowledge him: *"Thanks, (Sean). You certainly were strong to try so hard over and over again to walk the balance beam without falling off."*

Conduct a review (optional) by saying:

"Let's see how well we can remember. Some (or all) of us told about something we couldn't do and were finally able to do after we tried again and again. Who remembers what (Sean) told us he could do after trying again and again? Raise your hand."

Call on individual children to tell each other what they heard each other say and as they do this accurately, reinforce them: *"How well you listened to (Sean), (Mark). Now, does anybody remember what kinds of feelings (Sean) said he had when he was finally able to walk the balance beam without falling off?"* Reinforce again those who remember specific feelings reported. Continue until all of the children have been reviewed to. Be sure to ask a child to review to you too.

Lead a summary by asking:

1. *"When we can't do something we really want to do, what must we do so we can finally succeed?"*

2. *"How does it make us feel when we don't give up and are finally able to do what we wanted because we kept trying."*

As much as possible, in free-flowing discussion, allow the children to supply responses to these questions themselves. Guide them to recognize that everyone faces situations in which they must keep trying to do something in order to succeed. We can say to ourselves: *"Self, just keep trying. Sooner or later you will do it!"* Additionally emphasize the point that it's worth it when we do this because we can rightly take pride in ourselves. We can tell ourselves: *"Good for you!"*

Conclude the Magic Circle:

Thank the children for sharing and listening so well to make the circle a success.

Magic Circle Topic:

"A Time I Did It All By Myself"

Purpose:

This Magic Circle directly addresses a key developmental issue in the lives of young children: becoming more independent. It affords each child the opportunity to build his own self-esteem, self-confidence, and self-efficacy by mentally identifying a time when he functioned independently and then telling others about it. In the process he is enabled to gain many ideas along these lines from his peers.

Introduce the Topic:

Tell the children in your own words: *"Our topic for this Magic Circle is: 'A Time I Did It All By Myself.' There are many times in our lives when we need to have other people help us do things. But there are other times when it is better to be able to do things all by ourselves. Today we will have a chance to tell each other about a time when we did do something all by ourselves. Can you think of a time when you did something with no one's help? It could have been the first time you got dressed all by yourself. It could have been a time when you fixed something to eat all by yourself. Or maybe it was the first time you rode your trike alone."*

"Let's close our eyes and think. Can you remember a time when you were able to do something all by yourself? Just think for a moment or two. When you're ready to tell us about something you did all by yourself, open your eyes and look at me. Then I'll know you are ready to talk and listen."

Involve the children:

Demonstrate that you are thinking about the topic by closing your eyes and concentrating for several seconds. Invite the children to take turns to speak. If no one is ready, take your turn first. You could say something like this: *"When I was (five) years old I was scared to walk to school all by myself. My house was about three blocks away from the school. So my mother used to walk with me to school and then come and get me when school was over. That meant she had to take the walk twice. One day she asked me to help her out by taking the walk to school and home again all by myself. That way she could get more done at home. I wanted to help her out but I was still scared, but I tried it anyway. Well, you know, I did it fine the first time. I was a little nervous, but I was okay walking by myself. Then I just kept on doing it day after day and before long I knew I'd never need her to walk with me to school again. I felt so proud and grown up!"*

Invite the children to take turns to speak: *"Who would like to tell us about something you did all by yourself? Raise your hand if you are ready."* As necessary, ask open-ended questions to individual children as they share, but do so sparingly: *"How did you learn to tie your shoes, (Bill)?" "Tell us how you feel when you do it all by yourself?"* As each child completes his remarks, thank him for his contribution: *"Setting the table all by yourself certainly was an accomplishment, (Joey). Thank you for telling us about it!"*

Conduct a review (optional) by saying:

"Let's see how well we can remember. Some (or all) of us told about a time we did something all by ourselves. Who remembers what (Bill) told us about? Raise your hand."

Proceed in this manner, directing the children to tell each other what they heard each other say. Reinforce them for their correct reflections: *"How well you listened to (Bill), (Sharon)! You didn't forget he told us he tied his shoes all by himself this morning. Now, does anybody remember what kind of feelings (Bill) said he had when he was able to do it?"* Reinforce again those who remember specific feelings reported. Continue until all of the children have been reviewed to. Be sure to include yourself in the review.

Lead a summary by asking:

1. *"What were we able to do in our Magic Circle today?"*
2. *"Is it good to be able to do things all by ourselves? Why?"*

As much as possible, in free-flowing discussion, allow the children to supply responses to these questions themselves. Affirm their understanding that each child who shared was able to tell about one way to do something all by him/herself. Emphasize the points that doing things all by ourselves frees up the people who used to have to do them for us which makes them feel good; it also gives us the right to feel proud of ourselves because now we are more grown up. We can say to ourselves: *"Good for you, self. You did that all by yourself!"*

Conclude the Magic Circle:

Thank the children for doing such a good job of listening and sharing in the circle today.

Related Activity:

Ask the children to draw pictures of themselves doing the things they learned to do all by themselves. Post their pictures on a bulletin board or large folding cardboard display with captions telling about the artist and his behavior. For example.

Bill can tie his shoes all by himself.

Joey sets the table all by himself, etc.

Gather the children together the next day to view the display with you. Look at each picture and point out something positive about it. Read each caption to the children and then ask them to read it with you aloud.

Magic Circle Topic:

"A Time My Mistake Helped Me Learn"

Purpose:

This Magic Circle affords each child the opportunity to learn that success is frequently won as a result of corrective action. Each child may tell about a time when a mistake was his teacher. In the process he is enabled to deduce that guilt and shame over a mistake are unhelpful reactions. Moreover, he may recognize that fear of making mistakes in the future should not preclude attempting new activities.

Introduce the topic:

Tell the children in your own words: *"Today we are going to have a chance to tell each other about something we were able to learn because the first time we tried it we got it wrong and that helped us figure out how to do it right. Our topic is: 'A Time My Mistake Helped Me Learn.'*

"Have you ever noticed how hard it is to do some things right the very first time you try them? There are so many things like that. Of course, no one ever wants to make a mistake and we shouldn't make mistakes on purpose, but often it is only after we have made a mistake that we find out how to do something better the next time. When you learn how to do something from a mistake that's an accomplishment!

"Think for a bit about something you learned to do because your mistake helped you learn. Maybe it was something like finally learning how to tie your shoes after you made some mistakes at first. Or perhaps you learned not to touch things on the stove because once when you did it, you got burned. If you would like to tell us about a time you learned something from a mistake you made, we would like to hear about it. Let's close our eyes and think. When you open them I'll know you are ready to talk and listen."

Involve the children:

Demonstrate that you are thinking about the topic by closing your eyes and concentrating for several seconds. Invite the children to raise their hands when they are ready to share. If they are not ready, take your turn first. You might say something like this: *"I've thought of something I did wrong at first when I was (three) years old. The first time I tried to button my shirt I put the wrong buttons and buttonholes together and when my mother saw me she started laughing. She said she really liked it that I had tried, but then she took me to the mirror and showed me how I had done it wrong. Then we laughed together. We unbuttoned my shirt and she helped me get started doing it right. We did the first button together and then I did the rest all by myself. After that I usually buttoned my own shirt, or blouse, each day and I was careful to get it started right.*

"Now, who would like to tell us about a time when your mistake helped you learn how to do something right?" As the children speak, model effective listening skills.

As necessary, assist each one with the use of open-ended questions: *"Tell us about the mistake, Susan." "What was it like for you when you found out you had gotten it wrong?" "How did you feel when you got it right?"* As each child completes his turn, acknowledge his contribution: *"Thanks (Davey). We appreciate hearing how you learned to keep your glass of milk away from the edge of the table so you wouldn't knock it over."*

Conduct a review (Optional) by saying:

"Let's see how well we listened to each other. Who can remember what (Susan's) mistake was and

what she learned? Raise your hand." Guide the children to tell each other what they heard each other say in this manner, asking also about the feelings the children remember hearing each other report.

Reinforce the children for their listening abilities: *"Good for you, (Susan)! You remembered what (Davey) told us."* Be sure everyone who shared during the circle is reviewed to, including yourself.

Lead a summary by asking:

1. *"What did we talk about in our Magic Circle today?"*
2. *"We usually think of mistakes as bad things. Is there anything good about a mistake?"*
3. *"Should we let our fear of making a mistake keep us from trying new things?"*

As much as possible, in free-flowing discussion, allow the children to supply responses to these questions themselves. Affirm their understanding that they told about the accomplishment of learning something from one of their own mistakes. Help them understand that mistakes are sometimes our best teachers and it is sad when we let fear keep us from trying things because we might get it wrong the first time we try. We can say to ourselves: *"Self, you made a mistake. What can it teach you?"* Then, when we get it right we can say to ourselves: *"Good for you, self. You learned from your mistake!"*

Conclude the Magic Circle:

Thank the children for sharing and listening so well to make the circle a success.

Related Activity:

Both before and after this Magic Circle conduct several informal sessions with the children about how shoes are tied; zippers zipped; buttons, buttoned; belts buckled; etc., using shoes with laces and items of clothing with zippers, buttons and buckles, etc. Demonstrate for the children; then allow them to experiment and practice. Talk about how getting it wrong at first helps us learn what not to do, and because we continue to practice the right way, we can get it right more often.

Unit IX

Social Development and Responsibility

Understanding and Caring for Each Other

Social responsibility depends on empathy. An individual's kind and considerate behavior has, as its basis, his genuine ability to find within himself the feelings another might have and to care about the other's emotional experience. One of the greatest gifts counselors, teachers and parents can instill within new generations is this powerful interpersonal quality and its demonstration in everyday life.

While some small children are capable of remarkable shows of giving, most need to be socialized, or trained, to care about another person's feelings and to behave with those feelings in mind. When adults discuss how they care about others and model empathy-backed behavior, they make a profound impact on children. Adults can also teach children to behave empathically by bringing interpersonal issues to their attention and talking with them about these issues. At such times adults can help the child learn to have respect for others and to care about other peoples' feelings. They can also teach the child about the reciprocity of human nature; ethically responsible behavior shown to others is the best choice because ultimately it benefits those who behave in ethically responsible ways.

A major theme of the Magic Circle is the repetitive performance of empathic behavior as set forth in the Magic Circle Promises. Additionally, this unit focuses directly on the fact that people affect each other emotionally. Specifically, it brings to the children's articulate awareness that people and animals have feelings just like they do, and they have the power to affect those feelings by their actions. Additionally, the child is enabled to explore how many of his actions directly affect his own general well-being, including his feelings. He comes to care about feelings in others and in himself and to discover that he is an actor, not simply a reactor, in the human drama.

Magic Circle Topics for Unit Nine

"An Animal Liked What I Did"

"A Person Liked What I Did"

"Things People Do that Hurt Others"

"Things People Do to Create Anger in Others"

"How I Stay Safe at Home"

"How I Stay Safe Away from Home"

Magic Circle Topic:

"An Animal Liked What I Did"

Purpose:
This Magic Circle is designed to bring to the children's awareness their power to affect others emotionally and to care about their feelings. By solely discussing their positive actions toward animals reinforcement occurs, leaving negative behavior unreinforced.

Materials needed:
The picture "An Animal Liked What I Did," on page 106.

Introduce the topic:
Tell the children in your own words: *"Today we're going to do something very important in our Magic Circle. We're going to think and talk about how powerful you are. Did you know that you are powerful? (The children respond.) Yes, indeed you do have power! You can make an animal feel good or bad. Did you know that? In fact, our topic for this Magic Circle is: 'An Animal Liked What I Did.'*

"You know, animals are a lot like people. They have feelings just like we do and what people do to animals causes them to feel good or bad. How many of you have seen an animal and you knew he was feeling good; you could just tell? (The children respond.) And how many have seen an animal and you knew he was feeling bad? (The children respond.) I have a picture I'd like to show you and I'd like you to tell me how the animal is feeling." Present the picture and discuss it with the children, in terms of how the dog is feeling and why.

Ask the children: *"Let's think about things we have done to make an animal feel good. Maybe you have given a thirsty dog some water, like the boy in our picture. Or maybe you have done something else. Close your eyes and think about it for a minute. See if you can remember something you have done that an animal liked. If you would like to tell us about it, we would like to hear. When you're looking up at me, I'll know you are ready to discuss this topic."*

Involve the children:
Demonstrate that you are thinking about the topic yourself. Wait for a few moments and then ask: *"Who would like to tell us about something you did that an animal liked?"* As the children individually take their turns, assist them no more than necessary by asking open-ended questions: *"Tell us about the animal." "In what way did you (play with him)?" "How do you know he liked it?" "How did you feel about doing that?"* Etc. Be sure to thank each child for her contribution.

Conduct a review (optional), by asking:
"Who remembers what (Omar) told us about? If you do, raise your hand. If I call on you tell (Omar) as we listen." Guide the children to tell each other what they heard each other say in a direct manner as opposed to talking about the individual to the group.

Reinforce the children for listening so well to each other: *"Good job, (Rhonda), you listened very carefully. You remembered what (Omar) told us. Who remembers what he said about the feelings his dog seemed to have and how he felt when they went for a walk?"* Reinforce again those who remember the specific feelings reported. Be sure everyone who shared during the session is reviewed to, including yourself.

Lead a summary by asking:
1. *"What kind of power did we talk about having in this Magic Circle?"*
2. *"Why do people use their power to make an animal feel good instead of using it in a way that would make it feel bad?"*

As much as possible, in free-flowing discussion, allow the children to supply responses to these questions themselves. Affirm their understanding that they told about times they used their power to make an animal feel good. This power works through actions; it is the way they treated the animals that gave the animals good feelings. People use their power to make an animal feel good, instead of bad, because they care about the animal. They care how he feels. They know if they were the animal it would certainly matter to them if people cared how they felt and treated them in kind ways.

Conclude the Magic Circle:

Thank the children for sharing and listening so well as this important topic was discussed.

Related Activity:

Ask the children to draw a picture of themselves doing the things they told about in the Magic Circle that made an animal feel good. After posting their completed pictures on a bulletin board, or foldout cardboard display, focus on each picture as a group. Ask each child to talk about his picture. As the children speak, write down one sentence each one says verbatim. Later, make captions of these sentences and place the appropriate one under each child's picture. The next day, refocus the children's attention on the display and read each caption with them. Then ask the children to read each one with you aloud.

"An Animal Liked What I Did"

Magic Circle Topic:
"A Person Liked What I Did"

Purpose:

This Magic Circle is designed to bring to the children's awareness their power to affect the feelings of other people and to care how others feel. By solely discussing their positive actions toward people reinforcement occurs, leaving negative behavior unreinforced.

Materials needed:

The picture "A Person Liked What I Did," on page 109

Introduce the topic:

Tell the children in your own words: *"Do you remember what we talked about in our last Magic Circle? (The children respond.) Right! We talked about how we have used our power to make animals feel good. Today, in this Magic Circle, we're going to talk again about our power. Today we will talk about how we use this power to act in ways that bring about good feelings in people. Our topic is 'A Person Liked What I Did.'"*

"Many times in our Magic Circles we have talked about how people affect each other. We have noticed how the things they do affect our feelings and how the things we do affect their feelings. Can you think of a time when you did something to someone, or for someone, and he, or she, felt good about it? I have another picture to show you today. Let's look at it and see what it shows us." Present the picture and discuss it with the children, in terms of how the woman with the baby is feeling about the boy and girl who are helping her after she dropped some of her groceries.

Ask the children: *"Let's think about things we have done to someone, or for someone, that he, or she, liked. Maybe you helped someone when they needed help like the boy and girl in the picture. Or maybe you said something friendly to someone and he, or she, felt good about it. Close your eyes and think about it for a minute. See if you can remember something you have done that someone liked. If you want to tell us about it, we would like to hear. When you're looking up at me, I'll know you are ready to share and listen to what others have to say."*

Involve the children:

Demonstrate that you are thinking about the topic yourself. Wait for a few moments and then ask: *"Who would like to tell us about something you did that a person liked?"* As the children individually take their turns, assist them no more than necessary by asking open-ended questions: *"Tell us about what happened." "In what way (were you nice to him, or her)?" "How do you know he liked what you did?" "How did you feel about doing that?"* Etc. Be sure to thank each child for his contribution.

Conduct a review (optional), by asking:

"Who remembers what (Elizabeth) told us? If you do, raise your hand. If I call on you tell her as we listen." Guide the children to tell each other what they heard each other say in a direct manner.

Reinforce the children for listening so well to each other: *"Very nice reviewing (Reggie), you listened to (Elizabeth) very well. You remembered she told us she put her arms around her friend when her friend was crying. Does anyone remember how (Elizabeth) knew her friend liked that and how she felt about herself for doing it?"* Reinforce again those who remember the specific feelings reported. Be sure everyone who shared during the session is reviewed to, including yourself.

Lead a summary by asking:

1. *"What kind of power did we talk about having in this Magic Circle?"*

2. *"What causes people to use their power in kind ways instead of unkind ways?"*

As much as possible, in free-flowing discussion, allow the children to supply responses to these questions themselves. Affirm their understanding that they told about times they used their power to do something someone felt good about. This power works through actions; it is the way the children treated the people that gave those people good feelings. We use our power in kind ways, instead of unkind ways, because we care about the other person. We care how he, or she, feels. We know if we were the other person it would matter a lot to us if he, or she, cared about us and treated us in kind ways.

Conclude the Magic Circle:

Thank the children for sharing and listening so well as this important topic was discussed.

Related Activity:

Suggest to the children that each one finds ways to be kind to the other children during the rest of the day. Before going home have a short feedback period in which you invite them to say thank you to someone who was kind to them. Demonstrate by going first. For example: *"I want to thank Jessa for opening the door for us when we came back into the room from outdoor play."* After all of the children who wish to thank another child have had a turn, make your own statements of thanks to those who were not mentioned by other children. Be sure everyone receives some acknowledgment.

"A Person Liked What I Did"

Magic Circle Topic:

"Things People Do that Hurt Others"

Purpose:

After having focused in the two prior sessions on how they have personally affected animals and people positively by their actions, this Magic Circle allows the children to discuss behavior that hurts others. This discussion occurs in a hypothetical vein and does not center around the children's actual deeds. In this non-threatening atmosphere, devoid of public confessions, children are enabled to make judgments for themselves about the undesirability of unkind behavior.

Materials needed:

The picture "Things People Do that Hurt Others," on page 112.

Introduce the topic:

Tell the children in your own words: *"In our last two Magic Circles we talked about the power we have to do things that animals and people like. We told about kind things we did ourselves because we cared about the animals and the people. Today our topic is about this power we all have, but today we are going to talk about times when it can be used in harmful ways. Our topic is, 'Things People Do that Hurt Others.'*

"I have another picture to show you today. Let's take a look at it." Present the picture and discuss it with the children, in terms of how the girl probably feels about having her braid yanked by the boy. Point out that the boy is not a bad person, just a person who is doing a bad thing. He's probably doing it because he doesn't care how she feels.

Suggest: *"There are other things people can do to hurt other people. Let's see if we can think of what some of those things might be. I don't want you to tell us how you might have hurt someone. That isn't necessary. Just think about things you know of that people can do to other people that those people wouldn't like. Close your eyes and think about it for a minute. See if you can remember something you have seen someone do that hurt someone else. If you want to tell us about it, we would like to hear, but don't tell us who the people were. Don't tell us their names. When you're looking up at me, I'll know you are ready to share and listen to what others have to say."*

Involve the children:

Demonstrate that you are thinking about the topic yourself. Wait for a few moments and then ask: *"Who would like to tell us about something you have thought of that would hurt someone?"* This is a challenging topic and it is likely the children may not be ready to speak. If this occurs take your turn first. You might say something like this: *"I think it would hurt a person if he was talking to someone else and the person he was talking to just interrupted him in the middle of what he was saying. It would probably make him feel that the one he was talking to didn't care about his feelings. Can anyone think of something else a person could do to hurt another person?"*

As the children individually take their turns, assist them no more than necessary by asking open-ended questions: *"Tell us about your thought." "Tell us how the person would act?" "How would it probably make a person feel if someone did that to him?"* Etc. Due to the hypothetical nature of this topic, you may also need to help the children put their thoughts into words. Do this no more than absolutely necessary, however. Be sure to thank each child for his contribution.

Lead a summary by asking:

1. *"Did we talk about power people have in this Magic Circle?"*

2. *"What causes people to use their power in unkind ways sometimes?"*

3. *"How do we feel when someone uses their power in unkind ways?... In kind ways?*

As much as possible, in free-flowing discussion, allow the children to supply responses to these questions themselves. Affirm their understanding that they told about things people do that hurt other people. This is the same power people have to be kind only it's turned the other way. We can use our power to be kind or unkind; we use it with our actions. Many times people are unkind to others because they *don't care* how those other people feel. They don't think to themselves: *if I were him and he did this, it would hurt me, so I won't do it to him.*

Conclude the Magic Circle:

Thank the children for sharing and listening so well as this important topic was discussed.

"Things People Do that Hurt Others"

Magic Circle Topic:

"Things People Do to Create Anger in Others"

Purpose:

This Magic Circle allows the children to discuss behavior that arouses anger in others. This discussion occurs in a hypothetical vein and does not center around the children's actual deeds. In this non-threatening atmosphere, devoid of public confessions, children are enabled to make judgments for themselves about the undesirability of behaving in ways that arouse anger in others.

Materials needed:

The picture "Things People Do to Create Anger in Others," on page 115.

Introduce the topic:

Tell the children in your own words: *"Who remembers what we talked about in our last Magic Circle? (The children respond.) That's right! We talked about things people do that hurt other people. We discussed how people often hurt others when they don't care how those other people feel. Today our topic is similar, but not quite the same. It is: 'Things People Do to Create Anger in Others.'*

"Let's take a look at the picture I have to show you today." Present the picture and discuss it with the children, in terms of how the boy who was building a tower with blocks undoubtedly feels about the other boy kicking it down. Talk about the anger the boy with the blocks obviously feels. Acknowledge that the boy who is kicking is probably angry too. He is mad at the boy he is upsetting and wants to hurt him, or maybe he is mad at someone else, and just doesn't care how he makes the boy with the blocks feel.

Suggest: *"There are other things people do to make other people angry. Let's see if we can think of what some of those things might be. I don't want you to tell us how you might have made somebody mad. That isn't necessary. Just think about things you know of that people can do to other people that would probably make those people angry. Close your eyes and think about it for a minute. See if you can remember something you have seen someone do that got someone else mad. If you want to tell us about it, we would like to hear, but don't tell us who the people were. Don't say their names. When you're looking up at me, I'll know you are ready to speak and listen."*

Involve the children:

Demonstrate that you are thinking about the topic yourself. Wait for a few moments and then ask: *"Who would like to tell us about something you have thought of that would probably create anger in a person?"* This is a challenging topic and it is likely the children may not be ready to speak. If this occurs take your turn first. You might say something like this: *"I know it would create anger in a person if someone else took something from him and ran away with it. That would probably make him feel very upset. He would feel like the person who stole from him didn't care at all about his feelings. Can anyone think of something else a person could do to create anger in another person?"*

As the children individually take their turns, assist them no more than necessary by asking open-ended questions: *"Tell us about your thought." "Tell us how the person would act?" "How would it probably make a person feel if someone did that to him?"* Etc. Due to the hypothetical nature of this topic, you may also need to help the children put their thoughts into words. Be sure to thank each child for his contribution.

Conduct a review (optional), by asking:

"Who remembers what (Bobby's) thought was? If you do, raise your hand. If I call on you tell him as we listen." Guide the children to tell each other what they heard each other say in a direct manner.

Reinforce the children for listening so well to each other: *"Yes, (Fred), you certainly listened to (Bobby). You remembered he said it would make a person mad if another person tripped him and then laughed as he fell down."* Be sure everyone who shared during the session is reviewed to, including yourself.

Lead a summary by asking:

1. *"Did we talk about power people have in this Magic Circle?"*
2. *"What causes some people to use their power in such unkind ways sometimes?"*

As much as possible, in free-flowing discussion, allow the children to supply responses to these questions themselves. Affirm their understanding that they told about things people do that anger other people. Many times one person does something to make someone else mad because he, himself, is angry. He may be angry at the person he hurts or at someone else and so he just lashes out without thinking. Everybody gets mad at times. The important thing to remember is that lashing out at another person only makes things worse. It's best to admit to ourselves that we are angry and find something else to do with the energy our anger is giving us instead of lashing out at someone.

Conclude the Magic Circle:

Thank the children for sharing and listening so well as this important topic was discussed.

"Things People Do to Create Anger in Others"

Magic Circle Topic:

"How I Stay Safe at Home"

Purpose:

This Magic Circle enables the children to understand that they are important to the people who love them and to themselves. Because they are important there are serious dangers they need to be reminded of in order to avoid them. Today each child may mention one way he cares for himself by avoiding a certain danger at home. As this process unfolds he gains several reminders of other dangers to avoid from his peers.

Materials needed:

The pictures "How I Stay Safe at Home," on pages 118 and 119.

Introduce the topic:

Tell the children in your own words: *"Today our Magic Circle is going to be about things we never do because we want to stay safe. Our topic is: 'How I Stay Safe at Home.' But before we go any further, let me ask you a question: who takes care of you? (The children respond.) Yes, that's true. Your parents take care of you and other people like baby-sitters take care of you, but you take care of you too. And the older you get the more you won't need other people to do it. When people take care of themselves they do things for themselves and they keep from doing other things. They keep from doing dangerous things so they can stay safe. Let me show you a picture of a little boy who is not taking very good care of himself. Look at the picture and see if you can tell what he is doing that is not good for him."*

Present the first picture. Discuss with the children the sad thing that could happen next to this boy who is holding a dangerous chemical. Talk about what he should do instead in order to stay safe. Then present the next picture and talk about how the girl with her mother's pills might make a big mistake with them. Talk about why taking the pills herself could be such a big mistake. Point out that children who care about themselves and their parents don't make these kinds of mistakes unless they don't know any better.

Explain: *"You are very important children and your lives are precious. Let's talk about ways you know about to stay safe at home so nothing bad like this will ever happen to any of you. Each of you may tell us one dangerous thing you never do at home so you will stay safe. Close your eyes and think about it for a minute. If you want to share, we would like to hear what you have to say. When you're looking up at me, I'll know you are ready to speak and listen."*

Involve the children:

Demonstrate that you are thinking about the topic yourself. Wait for a few moments and then ask: *"Who would like to tell us about a way you stay safe at home?"* This is another challenging topic and it is likely the children may not be ready to speak. If this occurs take your turn first. You might say something like this: *"One way I stay safe at home is to keep my doors locked, especially when I'm home alone. That way a person who could harm me is less likely to be able to get in. Can anyone think of something you do at home in order to stay safe?"*

As the children individually take their turns, assist them no more than necessary by asking open-ended questions: *"Tell us how you keep from falling down the stairs?" "Tell us what could happen if you played with matches?" "How would you feel if you got burned?" How would your parents feel?"* Be ready to help the children put their ideas into words, but do this no more than absolutely necessary. Be sure to thank each child for his contribution.

Conduct a review (optional), by asking:

"Who remembers what (Cecilia) does at home to stay safe? If you do, raise your hand. If I call on you tell her as we listen." Guide the children to tell each other what they heard each other say in a direct manner.

Reinforce the children for listening so well to each other: *"(Frankie), you listened very well to (Cecilia). You remembered she said she stays safe at home by never tasting the things in the bottles in the medicine cabinet."* Be sure everyone who shared during the session is reviewed to, including yourself.

Lead a summary by asking:

1. *"Did we talk about our power again today in this Magic Circle?"*
2. *"Why is it important to stay safe?"*

As much as possible, in free-flowing discussion, allow the children to supply responses to these questions themselves. Affirm their understanding that they told about ways they know of to stay safe at home. Emphasize the point that they are grown up enough now to start taking good care of themselves. And because they are very important and much loved children by their parents, you, and themselves, they deserve to be taken care of by themselves very, very well. One of the best ways to do this is to keep themselves out of danger.

Conclude the Magic Circle:

Thank the children for sharing and listening so well as this important topic was discussed.

Related Activities:

To underscore the key concepts of this Magic Circle, create a chant with the children, inserting the ways they avoid danger at home. It could go something like this:

> We stay safe at home!
> We stay safe at home!
> Cecilia never takes medicine from the cabinet!
> That's how she stays safe at home! Etc.

Send a letter home to the children's parents telling them about this Magic Circle and the next one. Suggest in the letter they have a friendly conversation with their child about what was shared and learned.

"How I Stay Safe at Home"

"How I Stay Safe at Home"

Magic Circle Topic:

"How I Stay Safe Away from Home"

Purpose:

This Magic Circle enables the children to understand that they are important to the people who love them and to themselves. Because they are important there are serious dangers they need to be reminded of in order to avoid them. Today each child may mention one way he cares for himself by avoiding a certain danger when he is away from home. As this process unfolds he gains several reminders of other dangers to avoid from his peers.

Materials needed:

The picture series "How I Stay Safe Away from Home," on pages 122, 123, and 124.

Introduce the topic:

Tell the children in your own words: *"Do you remember what we talked about in our last Magic Circle? (The children respond.) Good for you. You remember that we talked about how we stay safe at home. All of you (or some of you) told about things you never do at home because they are dangerous and you want to take very good care of yourselves. That's because you are important to your parents, to me, and to yourselves. Today our topic is similar but not the same. Today we will talk about the ways we take care of ourselves when we are not inside our houses. The topic is: 'How I Stay Safe Away from Home.'*

"Let me show you two pictures of children doing something very unsafe." Present the first picture. Discuss with the children how the boy chasing the ball into the street could easily be hit by the car. (Note that the driver is very upset because he can't do anything to avoid it.) Ask the children what the boy should have done instead when his ball bounced out into the street. Then present the second picture and discuss how there have been some people who seemed so nice and friendly to children and invited them to get into their cars, but it was a big mistake when those children got in. Without frightening the children unduly, make sure they understand that terrible consequences could occur if they got into a car with someone except for their parents or people their parents have said are okay to ride with.

Finally, present the last picture and tell the children: *"Now this boy and girl are doing something right. They are staying safe. How can we tell?"* Discuss all the things the children need to know in order to safely cross a street, including the word, "walk" and the picture of the person walking on the signal light.

Emphasize the point that children who care about themselves and their parents don't make these kinds of mistakes unless they don't know any better. As in the prior session, re-explain: *"You are very important children and your lives are precious. Let's talk about ways you know about to stay safe when you are not at home so nothing bad will ever happen to any of you. Each of you may tell us one way you stay safe when you are not inside your house or apartment. Close your eyes and think about it for a minute. If you want to share, we would like to hear what you have to say. When you're looking up at me, I'll know you are ready to speak and listen to what others have to say."*

Involve the children:

Demonstrate that you are thinking about the topic yourself. Wait for a few moments and then ask: *"Who would like to tell us about a way you stay safe when you are not at home."* This is another challenging topic and it is likely the children may not be ready to speak. If this occurs take your turn first. You might say something like this: *"There's a way I stay safe when I am not at home. I do not walk alone in places I don't know very well at night unless there are lots of lights and people around.*

Instead, I go with someone or I stay indoors. That's one way I stay safe. Can anyone think of something you do when you are not at home in order to stay safe?"

As the children individually take their turns, assist them no more than necessary by asking open-ended questions: *"Tell us how you keep from falling off your scooter?" "Tell us why you never go into the neighbor's swimming pool?" "How would you feel if you got lost at the store?" "How would your parents feel?"* Be ready to help the children put their ideas into words, but do this no more than absolutely necessary. Be sure to thank each child for his contribution.

Conduct a review (optional), by asking:

"Who remembers what (Ted) told us he doesn't do when he's not at home in order to stay safe?" If you do, raise your hand. If I call on you tell him as we listen." Guide the children to tell each other what they heard each other say in a direct manner.

Reinforce the children for listening so well to each other: *"Good listening, (Brenda)! You remembered that (Ted) told us he never goes into the woods all by himself."* Be sure everyone who shared during the session is reviewed to, including yourself.

Lead a summary by asking:

1. *"Did we talk about our power again today in this Magic Circle?"*

2. *"Why is it important to stay safe?"*

3. *"Why is it important to think about what you need to do to stay safe?*

In free-flowing discussion, allow the children to supply responses to these questions themselves.

Affirm their understanding that they told about ways they know of to stay safe when they are away from home. As in the prior session, emphasize the point that they are grown up enough now to start taking good care of themselves more and more. And because they are very important and much loved children by their parents, you, and themselves, they deserve to be taken care of by themselves very, very well. One of the best ways to do this is to keep themselves out of danger.

Conclude the Magic Circle:

Thank the children for sharing and listening so well as this important topic was discussed.

Related Activities:

To underscore the learnings of this Magic Circle, create a chant with the children, inserting the ways they avoid danger when they are not at home. It could go something like this:

> We stay safe... when we're away from home!
> We stay safe... when we're away from home!
> Ted never goes into the woods alone!
> That's how he stays safe... when he's away from home! Etc.

Send a letter home to the children's parents telling them about this Magic Circle and the prior one. Suggest in the letter they have a friendly conversation with their child about what was shared and learned.

"How I Stay Safe Away from Home"

"How I Stay Safe Away from Home"

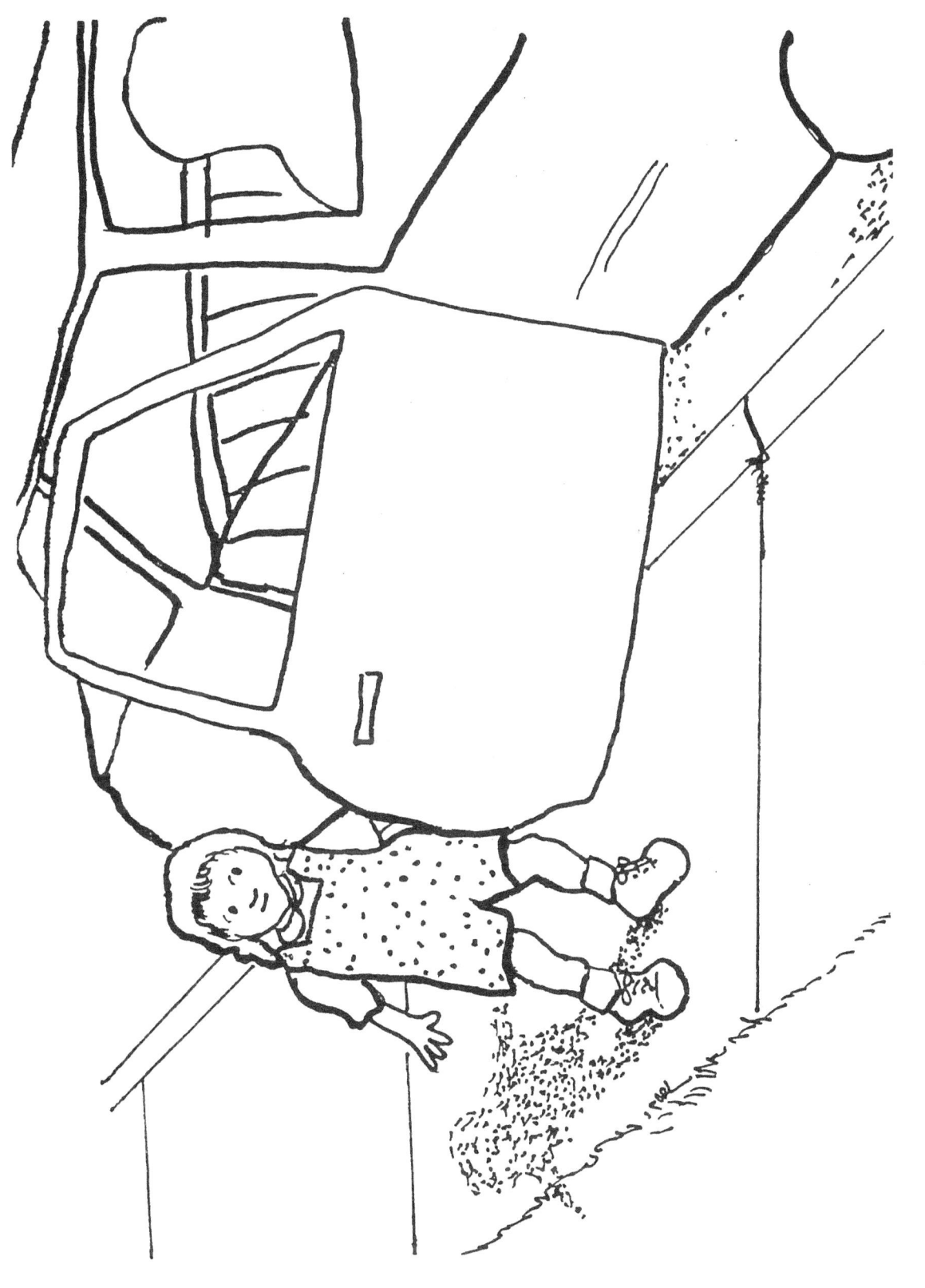

"How I Stay Safe Away from Home"

If your heart is in Social-Emotional
Learning, visit us online.

Come see us at
www.InnerchoicePublishing.com

Our web site gives you a look at all our other Social-Emotional Learning-based books, free activities, articles, research, and learning and teaching strategies. Every week you'll get a new Sharing Circle topic and lesson.

15079 Oak Chase Court
Wellington, FL 33414

www.ingramcontent.com/pod-product-compliance
Lightning Source LLC
Chambersburg PA
CBHW081940170426
43202CB00018B/2956